SOCIETY FOR
HUMAN
RESOURCE
MANAGEMENT

D1560438

GETTING STARTED IN
HUMAN RESOURCE MANAGEMENT

JOSEPH P. BACARRO, SR., SPHR

Action Management, Inc.
Overland Park, Kansas

SHRM FOUNDATION
SOCIETY FOR HUMAN RESOURCE MANAGEMENT

ISBN 0-939900-69-6

This book is published by the Society for Human Resource Management and was funded by a grant from the SHRM Foundation, generously supported by the Human Resource Certification Institute. The interpretations, conclusions, and recommendations, however, are those of the author, and do not necessarily represent SHRM or the SHRM Foundation.

Joseph P. Bacarro, SPHR, has more than 30 years of management, human resources, and consulting experience. He is a principal with Action Management, Inc. He provides practical management, human resource, and employee relations services to a broad range of clients. Mr. Bacarro is a long-time member of the Society for Human Resource Management and is the 1996 Chair of the SHRM Employee and Labor Relations Committee. He is a "subject matter expert" in employee relations and advises the SHRM Learning System Editorial Board on those issues.

CONTENTS

INTRODUCTION

This book is about designing a human resource function in a company. It provides easy-to-follow instructions on how to design a foundation for a reliable and productive employee relations strategy. The book identifies possible enhancements in the management practices of readers' companies compared with accepted standards and practices. It also discusses compliance with federal and state regulations that affect the management of human resources and suggests ways to make these regulations work for the company instead of against it.

Many companies with fewer than 100 employees do not have a human resource manager. Top management consists of a president and four or five other persons, each responsible for a particular aspect of the business: production, marketing, sales, accounting and distribution, research and development, and so forth. In many situations, there is a need for professional advice, but not necessarily for a full-time human resource person. Ongoing human resource activities and services can be provided through a mix of outsourcing; obtaining advice from experienced professionals, management consultants, or employee relations lawyers; and persuading managers to exercise good management practices.

Throughout this book, the terms "human resource function" and "human resource professional" are used instead of "human resource department." This is intentional, because many small and emerging companies should be developing human resource *processes*, not hiring someone to start a department. Starting a new human resource department in such companies often results in creating a "functional silo," in which it becomes the responsibility of human resource professionals, rather than company managers, to solve employee relations problems.

The processes and techniques discussed in this book are the result of 30 years of practical experience, formal education, and continuous self-directed learning. Experience as a salaried employee, union officer, line supervisor, human resource manager, law firm employee relations consultant, management consultant, and small business owner has led the author to certain convictions about the value of good management practices and the role of human resources in an organization. These convictions do not arise from blindly following the human resources philosophy of scientific management or the traditional model of management. If anything, experience has encouraged the author to question management practices that focus on short-term profits and the prevalent belief that success and profit must come as a result of the exploitation of others.

Readers may question specific advice offered in this book; suggestions or recommendations for improvement are sincerely welcome.

Many people helped in the publication of this book; without their support, encouragement, and advice, it would not have been possible. The author specifically wishes to thank Ms. Margaret Evans, SPHR, Director of Human Resources for Government Employees Hospital Association, for her assistance in outlining the topics to be covered. Mr. Arthur Ritter, President of Quality Advisors, provided valuable counsel and advice from the perspective of a small business owner who is not a human resource professional.

Chapter I

Essentials of Starting a Human Resource Function

This is a world in which decisions must be made quickly and implemented competently. The management of human resources (HR) is part of everyone's job. Decisions must be made when and where they occur at the line level; those closest to the action must know how to be firm and competent in carrying out their human resource responsibilities. They need to have expertise and to understand their responsibilities. With changing demographics and the increasingly complex legal environment, operating managers may find it difficult to do it all.

The human resource professional plays a critical role. Starting a human resource function requires more than reading a book, taking some classes, or attending a few legal seminars, yet many HR functions in small and emerging companies start this way.

This chapter provides an overview of (1) the responsibilities of a human resource professional, (2) strategic human resource planning and staffing, and (3) understanding the role of the HR generalist. It is intended to kindle a discussion of traditional HR activities while providing recommendations for such activities in a smaller organization.

Aspects of a Successful Human Resource Function

There are three important aspects to starting a successful human resource function. First, the HR professional must develop a sense of the value of human resource activities in the company through proficiency, confidence, and innovation. Second, the company must follow policies and practices that focus on the full use of its human resources. Third, the human resource practitioner must be a model manager and leader, not an authoritarian or controller.

Figure I-1 presents a model of the natural flow of human resource management, beginning with the objectives of the company. The human resource professional builds a sense of confidence and value in

Figure I-1. Flowchart of Human Resource Management

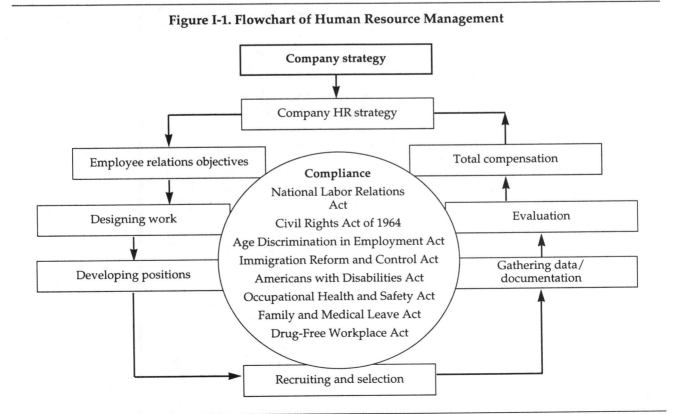

human resources by clearly linking employee personnel strategies to the objectives of the company. The flow chart demonstrates how human resource strategy is affected by compliance issues. (A summary of the federal laws affecting human resources is given in appendix B.)

In the past, programs and processes from one company could, with minor modifications, be applied to almost any other company. However, as companies and employees become more diverse, company strategies and human resource activities must be tailored to fit their unique needs. The human resource professional must anticipate future changes and design employee relations processes that will adapt to them. This means that the company must adopt a human resource strategy.

Being strategic means that everyone must understand the needs of the company and must use those needs as the basis for all human resource practices and procedures. Strategic human resource management means that operations managers must also participate in developing the processes. It is not the human resource professional who drives the process, it is the operations managers.

Consultants who have facilitated business planning have found that surprisingly little strategic attention is placed on the "people" aspects of business. This is true in very large organizations and in the expanding small businesses. Managers in these companies routinely debate and decide functional questions such as capacity, inventory, sales, quality, new order processing, and financials. Yet, as important as these questions are, they do not provide the means of accomplishing company objectives. It is only through a well-thought-out human resource strategy that a company can accomplish its objectives.

The company can develop processes that improve the full use of its human resources. Skillful and innovative staff and succession planning, recruiting, selection, data analysis, reward and recognition, and advising on compliance with federal laws and judicial decisions are valuable management activities. These activities influence company profitability and efficiency. The company can develop a sense of the value of human resource activities if the HR professional can prove the importance of these activities.

Figure I-2 illustrates the customer service chain. If a company strategy is to reduce turnover, the human resource strategy must be to satisfy employees by activities such as an improved communication process and increased career and job training, and better qualified managers. The cost of turnover will be reduced and the savings can be used to improve, strengthen, and accomplish other business objectives. Employees will be informed and able to provide better customer service. This focus on external quality will affect customer satisfaction and customer retention. Customer retention reduces waste and unnecessary expenses and provides the resources for continuous improvement and internal quality activities. These activities create more money for education and employee relations activities, which result in employee satisfaction. Focusing on human resources and employee relations improves overall business profitability and creates a good work environment.

Figure I-2. Customer Service Chain

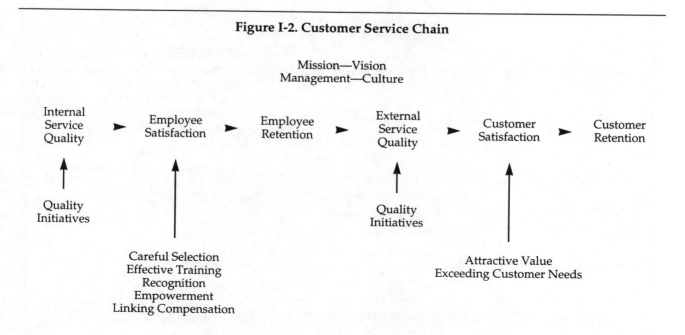

The human resource professional must be a model leader and manager. Understanding human resources is only one aspect of the role; being proficient at traditional management functions is another. The human resource professional should also function as a key confidential advisor to the chief executive officer (CEO). The job of operating a function, sticking to budgets, showing that activities are profitable, and recognizing the long-range implications of management decisions may conflict with the more important role of advising the CEO. The human relations professional can analyze the strengths and weaknesses of projects, positions, or activities in which the people factor may have been overlooked.

The human resource professional must have the tenacity to advance employee relations strategies during the planning of all strategic activities that affect employees. This might include the following:

- Advising management on the feasibility of acquisitions or downsizing.
- Identifying employee relations implications of plant relocations.
- Advocating appropriate selection requirements for top management.
- Championing workforce diversity as a competitive strategy.
- Discussing compensation and benefits limitations.
- Implementing safety and workers' compensation programs.
- Sponsoring productivity improvement or quality processes.
- Estimating the effect of remaining union-free.

Each of the above activities has implications for employee relations. However, HR practitioners usually do not participate at the strategic management level. For example, decisions on plant relocations are not considered people issues, but are made on the basis of tax advantages or other financial incentives.

Even with the focus on quality, human resources seldom participates fully in planning and implementing total quality changes. Instead, it is expected to provide training programs, suggest ways of tying compensation to quality, and help eliminate or, conversely, empower employees. None of these activities are the key to success. However, an experienced, knowledgeable human resource professional, armed with the right techniques, can lead the company in the right direction.

Mark Twain is reputed to have said, "It's not what we don't know that causes the problem; it's what we think we know and don't." This applies when managers rely on common sense, experience, and a limited knowledge of the legal constraints and practical techniques of managing people. If the owner or company manager acts from his or her own perspective, that perspective becomes reality, at least for him or her. Human resources should provide a reality check.

Human Resource Strategy and Its Relationship to Business Objectives

In recent years, enormous changes have taken place in the roles and responsibilities of what used to be called the Personnel Department. One change affecting the human resource function is the strategic planning process. Strategic planning is a process that begins with an assessment of the organization, commonly called a SWOT (strengths, weaknesses, opportunities, threats) analysis. A strategic planning questionnaire is included at the end of this chapter (**HRI-1.FRM**). The process yields (1) a *strategic or long-range business plan* based on internal capabilities and external dynamics and (2) an *operational or short-term plan* based on goals and objectives to be pursued immediately. *Human resource strategic planning* adds an emphasis on staff planning, management succession, training, job design, and other issues that shape human resource availability, efficiency, and use.

The companies best able to deal with change will be those with a human resource professional who thinks in strategic terms. The forces converging on business and HR include the following:

- Major demographic shifts that result in an aging, diverse, and shrinking workforce.
- Low basic skills of entry-level workers and a decrease in the supply of qualified and competent employees.
- A need for higher levels of job skills and for greater flexibility.
- More laws and more regulation of a company's discretion to operate a business.
- An emphasis on value-added, bottom-line responsibility for HR functions.

Long-Range Planning

The specifics vary by company, industry, and competitive environment. However, human resources should become involved in the company's strategic or long-range planning process.

Such plans address the following:

- Defining and developing the right kind of employee at all levels of the organization.
- Providing or finding the necessary training and development programs for skills enhancement and for creating an atmosphere of trust and commitment.
- Retaining people through programs that build loyalty and a sense of community among employees.
- Developing fair, flexible, competitive compensation and benefit programs that meet legal requirements and encourage employee retention.
- Creating performance appraisal systems that are based on organizational objectives and that reward contributions to the organization.
- Evaluating managerial potential to identify the leadership and professional qualities needed in the future according to the strategic plan.
- Offering career management programs that merge the goals of the organization with those of the individual.
- Providing a management succession planning system that ensures management continuity.

A common approach in human resource strategic planning is an internal focus; that is, meeting human resource availability requirements through internal resources. The premise is that the people needed to meet future strategic and operational demands exist within the organization or can be developed by the company. This internal focus is often the most cost-effective. It is a reliable path to obtaining the required skills and talents. The human resource professional who understands this approach can better position the company to find skilled workers when they are needed.

Key Concepts: Work Requirements, Staffing, and Efficiency

Position development and the staffing process are discussed in detail in chapter II. Human resource professionals should look at work requirements, staffing, and efficiency as a strategy that contributes to achieving company objectives and profitability. Many companies are inefficient and unproductive because they do not focus activities only on what adds value to their customers. The media are full of stories of companies, large and small, that are downsizing their workforces, cutting services, outsourcing operations, and closing facilities. It was not unfair competition that caused them to do this. When these companies could pass the inefficiencies and waste on to the customer, there was no need to be "lean and mean." However, today only those operations that are absolutely necessary can be justified. Human resources can play a significant role in achieving that objective. Two overall HR strategies can keep a company productive and efficient: (1) maintain efficient, full-time positions and (2) hire people who meet the essential qualifications for the job.

Maintain Only Full Positions

Hire only when the organization has a good business reason to do so. Is this job necessary? What would happen if the employee never came to work for the company? What would happen if the job being filled was abolished? Is it a real, full-time job? The answer often is that the departing employee was not really necessary and that nothing would happen if the new employee were not added. Why is it important that employees have a full job? How can more effective work simplification methods and work improvement techniques reduce employee grievances and employee problems? The answer is simple.

An employee with less than a full job will quickly find things to do with the excess time. Much of this time-filling will be consumed with unproductive behavior and wasting the time of other employees. At the very least, the employee's work will expand to fill the time allocated to it.

Human resource professionals are no different. A colleague tells of a situation in which his manager requested two additional staff members. The department was doing so much that it could no longer provide effective human resource services. The CEO refused the request, declaring that there would be no hiring. He told the HR manager to find ways to get things done with the current staff.

The human resource staff reevaluated what they were doing; they identified essential activities and those requested by others. These additional activities often were not essential and added no value for customers. Ultimately, they found that more than 50 percent of their activities were being conducted for other departments or did not have to be done at all. They decided not to add any staff people.

Experience working with total quality management (TQM) processes, and to a lesser degree in reengineering projects, confirms that more than 80 percent of waste (cost of quality) is found in activity that adds no value to the company's business, but is required because "We have always done it that way."

The answers to these three questions can identify significant opportunities for improvement:

1. How does this position add measurable value to the product or service provided to the customer?
2. If the position could not be filled for some reason, how would the work be accomplished?
3. Who could accomplish the required tasks, with or without some modification or accommodation?

Hire People Who Meet the Essential Qualifications of the Job

Research and experience have shown that companies regularly overspecify credentials when advertising for positions. In preparing for litigation on an Equal Employment Opportunity Commission (EEOC) case, a legal consultant studied the job advertisements in a major Midwest newspaper. Although the consultant was searching for only a few specific job classifications, approximately 80 percent of the professional positions listed were filled by someone who did not have all the qualifications requested in the published advertisements. Even for hourly workers, where qualifications requested were basic, almost 20 percent of those hired did not have all the qualifications listed.

In working with classification and position description projects, consultants are often faced with managers who set unrealistically high education and experience requirements for their subordinates. When position descriptions were studied, the current employee usually was adequately performing the job, although he or she did not meet the qualifications. From an employee relations and legal perspective, the company cannot justify overstated position requirements.

The Human Resource Generalist

Fifteen years ago, the major criticism of personnel professionals was that they focused on day-to-day operations and did not see the "big picture." Now human resources is viewed as an important part of management and is increasingly counted among the more significant management functions. The change from basic personnel activities to progressive human resources has not come easily. Changes are made every day that require new practices in human resource management. However, the basic philosophy and organizational needs of companies have not changed that much.

The fundamental reasons companies start a human resource function are to reduce costs, comply with government regulations, and, to some extent, copy their competition's HR practices.

In a recent survey, CEOs saw human resource professionals as not contributing to the bottom line and as an expense to the company. The human resource function was not considered to be as effective as other operational areas.

Why? The answer lies in the fact that management has reinforced a reactive orientation to human resource activities that makes it difficult to develop and maintain the necessary creative, proactive management style. In many organizations, human resources is considered to cover compensation and salary administration, hiring and firing, training and safety, security, and employee facilities. One early assignment is the employment function. Employment personnel respond to job requests and are expected to find applicants who meet the needs of managers. Recruiters seldom question whether the job specifications are valid.

What if a new professional starts in the compensation and benefits area? The typical compensation system is highly structured and consists of slotting jobs into their allotted places by applying rules. A compensation analyst waits for a situation to surface and then applies a rule. This sort of activity, like employment, trains professionals to be reactive.

What if a new recruit starts in industrial relations? In industrial relations the emphasis is on waiting until someone has an issue to resolve. The thrust of contract negotiations is to avoid getting trapped in concessions. When the contract is drawn, the emphasis is again on applying rules. Situations are dealt with after they arise, in reaction to the demands and actions of others.

The background and nature of these activities are enough to produce reactive professionals. They also create specialties or "functional silos." Especially in large companies, human resource professionals often learned the trade by starting in one specialty and moving through a series of other assignments to master the discipline. Once a person is programmed to be a specialist, changing the orientation is difficult.

In business today, the practice of human resources cannot be broken into specialty areas. To do so spells disaster. For example, to develop a successful pay or benefits process requires an evaluation of the impact on other areas, which a compensation specialist may find difficult to do. Any changes in compensation programs must consider the employee relations climate and strategies, turnover rate, complaint and grievance process, promotion process, EEOC issues, diversity and affirmative action considerations, and legal and legislative issues.

A new workers' compensation or safety and accident prevention program cannot be developed in a vacuum. There are compensation issues, labor and employee relations links, legislative constraints, training and development problems, quality and productivity concerns, and even EEOC and diversity concerns. Starting a safety and accident prevention process without grasping how these other considerations affect business success can be disastrous.

In initiating a human resource function, the professional needs to have a generalist perspective. Especially in small organizations, if experience and training are not sufficient HR professionals should get assistance, a reality check. Many poor and ineffective policies, procedures, and practices are being used in companies today because they were implemented piecemeal. In these companies, operating managers and company owners often reproach the human resource function; however, the problem is usually not human resources, but the lack of a more comprehensive generalist view.

HRI-1.FRM

STRATEGIC PLAN

Objective One:	
Strategy A:	

Major Action Steps to Be Taken	Priority	Projected Completion Date	Actual Completion Date
1. _____	_____	_____	_____
2. _____	_____	_____	_____
3. _____	_____	_____	_____
4. _____	_____	_____	_____
5. _____	_____	_____	_____
6. _____	_____	_____	_____

SPECIFIC ACTION STEP

Description of Action to Be Taken: (from Overall Action Plan) _____

Specific Steps Required	Person Assigned	Projected Completion Date	Problems/ Delays Encountered	Actual Completion Date
1. _____	_____	_____	_____	_____
2. _____	_____	_____	_____	_____
3. _____	_____	_____	_____	_____
4. _____	_____	_____	_____	_____
5. _____	_____	_____	_____	_____

CHAPTER II

RECRUITMENT AND SELECTION

Probably no human resource discipline, except possibly performance evaluation, is more important to an overall HR strategy than the recruitment and selection process. And yet few management processes are more poorly structured and fraught with significant exposure to employee relations liability than hiring. It is the first function identified as a personnel and industrial relations responsibility. Managers hold scores of contrary beliefs concerning the steps required and the correct methods. Academics, business writers, consultants, lawyers, and the federal government have studied the process down to its most minor detail. The result has been scores of books and articles, yet managers still do not agree on one way to recruit and select employees. In this chapter, the characteristics of the hiring processes and its legal and practical implications are discussed.

The Changing Character of Hiring

The character of hiring has changed. Many employers continue to place advertisements in the local newspaper or put a sign in their window asking for employees. They may receive many applications or just a few. But seldom do they find good employees. Businesses trying to fill entry- to medium-level jobs sometimes have a hard time finding employees at any cost. Sometimes they have to open plants in new locations because the labor pool at their current location is depleted.

Businesses cannot count on the traditional sources of employees. With so many employers searching for employees, knowledgeable human resource professionals can help by cultivating new applicant sources and by doing a better job of retaining the people they have hired. They are finding applicants with minimum skills but a desire to work. They are funding education and skill-building programs so these new employees will be qualified to produce the work needed to keep the company competitive.

The Legal Side of Hiring

In recruiting and selection, a company needs awareness of the legal issues. Bad management practices and workplace abuses resulted in powerful unions and individual employees lobbying for legal protection. Now we have federal employment regulations that affect most employer practices and restrict the ability to control certain aspects of company operations. In addition to federal laws, employers have to contend with state and local laws that regulate recruiting, selection, hiring, and promotion.

These lawsuits support public policy that says companies should treat employees fairly and provide equal employment opportunity in the workplace. The primary focus is on preventing discrimination in employment and personnel actions and discouraging unfair employer work practices. Companies must operate within these parameters. The relevant federal legislation includes the following:

- The **Fair Labor Standards Act (FLSA) of 1938** is the broadest piece of employee relations legislation in the United States. It regulates the status of employees (versus independent contractors) and provides for a minimum wage and overtime unless the employee is exempt. (For more information, see *Federal Wage and Hour Laws* published by the SHRM. The **Equal Pay Act of 1963** is technically an amendment to FLSA and prohibits wage discrimination by requiring equal pay for equal work. A prima facie case occurs when an employee shows that she or he receives a lower wage than a member of the opposite sex for work that requires substantially the same skills, effort, and responsibilities under similar working conditions.

- The **Age Discrimination Employment Act of 1978 (ADEA)** prohibits discrimination in employment for persons 40 and over. Amendments in 1978 and 1986 first raised and then eliminated the age at which an employee could be forced to retire. This act covers all private and public employers with 20 or more employees, unions with 25 or more members, employment agencies, and apprenticeship and training programs.

- **Title VII of the Civil Rights Act of 1964** prohibits discrimination in all terms and conditions of employment (including pay and benefits) on the basis of race, religion, ethnic group, sex, or national origin. It requires that all persons of the same skills, seniority, and background be treated similarly. Title VII was amended in 1972, 1978, and 1991. The act makes specific employment practices unlawful.

If employers use non-job-related and discriminatory personnel practices, they are liable for the resulting employee relations liability. The 1972 amendment expanded coverage to include government and educational institutions and private sector employers with 15 or more employees. The 1978 amendment made it illegal to discriminate on the basis of pregnancy, childbirth, or related conditions. The 1991 amendments provide for jury trials and the right to seek compensatory and punitive damage awards for victims of intentional discrimination. Victims of race and national origin discrimination can sue for unlimited damages.

- The **Uniform Guidelines on Employee Selection (1978)**—guidelines for carrying out Title VII of the Civil Rights Act—state that selection policies or practices that have an adverse impact on the employment opportunities for any race, sex, or ethnic group are considered discriminatory—and therefore illegal—unless business necessity can justify them. It defines "adverse impact."

- The **Fair Credit Reporting Act (1970)** requires employers to inform applicants in writing that they will conduct an inquiry into the applicants' financial status. Applicants must be informed if they are denied employment because of information obtained during the inquiry and must be given the name and address of the third party who investigated them.

- The **Vocational Rehabilitation Act (1973)**, amended in 1980, prevents employment discrimination against people who have physical or mental disabilities. The act requires federal contractors who have contracts of more than $2,500 to "take affirmative action to employ and advance disabled individuals" at all levels of employment, including jobs at the executive level.

- The **Privacy Act (1974)** prohibits federal agencies from revealing certain information without permission from employees. The act gives employees the right to inspect records about themselves held by the federal government and to make corrections and copies.

- The **Immigration and Naturalization Act (1966)** covers the hiring of resident aliens and new or prospective immigrants. Under a more recent law, the **Immigration Reform and Control Act of 1986 (IRCA)**, every U.S. employer must require new hires to provide specific documents showing that they are who they claim to be and they have the legal right to work in the United States. The burden of verifying that a new employee is eligible to work in the United States falls on the employer. The employee must compete an Immigration Control Form I-9, and an authorized representative of the employer must verify that the information presented is correct.

- The **Americans with Disabilities Act of 1990 (ADA)** protects qualified individuals with disabilities from unlawful discrimination in employment, public services and transportation, public accommodations, and telecommunication services. Discrimination is prohibited against qualified individuals with a disability if they can do the essential job functions with reasonable proficiency. An employer must make *reasonable accommodations* (without compromising safety) for persons with disabilities unless doing so would place *undue hardship* upon the employer. The emphasized words may have different meanings with different employers.

- The **Drug-Free Workplace Act (1988)** mandates that firms that do business with the federal government must have written drug-use policies. Federal contractors with contracts of $25,000 or more must follow certain requirements to certify that they maintain a drug-free workplace.

- **Executive Order 11246** requires federal contractors with contracts of more than $10,000 to comply with Title VII: they must not discriminate on the basis of race, color, religion, sex, or national origin. In addition, federal contractors with contracts over $50,000 and 50 or more employees must develop a written affirmative action plan to increase the workforce participation of members of protected classes.

In addition to these federal laws, state and municipal regulations also limit employers' discretion in the hiring process.

Developing a Selection Process

If a company does not have enough applicants, the first step is to develop a comprehensive recruiting policy. The policy must be based on the qualities needed in every employee and be so clear that a picture can be drawn of the right applicant. In addition, the company should have clearly defined recruiting goals and should communicate these goals. The recruiting policy and goals should be based on the company's strategic plan. (See **Figure II-1**.)

Figure II-1. Recruiting and Selection Process

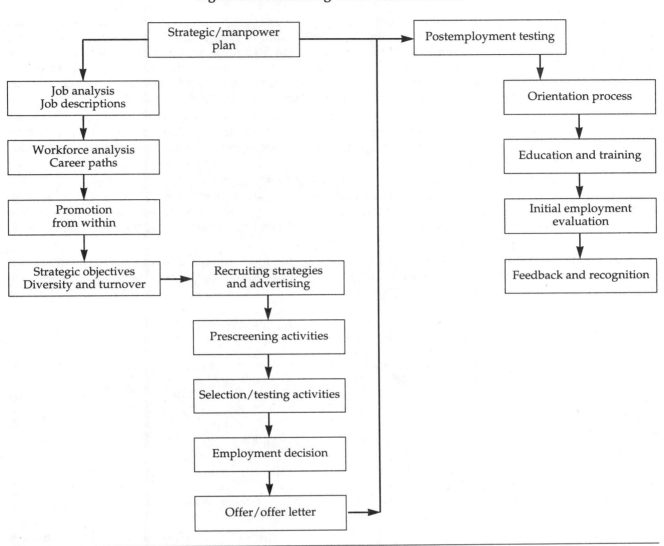

There are many sources from which to recruit applicants, depending on the company's recruiting and selection strategies and human resource objectives, the level of the vacant position, the number of positions to be filled, the availability of qualified applicants within a reasonable recruiting area, the culture of the company, and its employee relations practices.

When a position becomes vacant, many managers place an advertisement in the local newspaper. They make a major error and waste money and management resources trying to fill a position in this manner. The best approach is first to decide whether there is a full-time job and what the position will require in education and experience. Once a decision is made to fill the position, the hiring manager and human resources should agree on the recruiting strategy and the timetable for filling the position. The discussion should include a comprehensive review of current employees who may have the requisite skills or who could be trained to do the job.

If the position is hourly, nonexempt, or lower level management, many applicants can probably be found locally. Communicating the opening to current employees and their friends and relatives often produces a sufficient number of qualified applicants. Newspaper advertisements may garner additional applicants. However, the HR professional should take care that using these tactics does not result in an unbalanced workforce, either by gender or race.

In discrimination investigations, the Equal Employment Opportunity Commission (EEOC) uses statistics to find probable cause of illegal hiring practices. When there are disparities between the company's workforce composition and available applicants within a reasonable recruiting area, probable cause may exist.

Using referrals from current employees as the sole source of applicants can contribute to racial and gender imbalance.

Newspaper advertisements usually do not result in sufficient applications. The readership of mainstream newspapers in minority neighborhoods is often 10 percent of that in nonminority communities. While some companies use minority publications, the publishing dates and lead times required are often not consistent with a timely recruiting strategy. If the company wishes to increase its diversity regarding gender or the number of disabled employees, advocacy groups can be contacted. Nontraditional recruiting sources such as local "throwaway" publications and grocery store bulletin boards are often successful.

The company that is most successful in recruiting good employees locally has a recruiting policy integrated with its employee relations, marketing, and public relations strategies. The company is seen as a good place to work, with excellent people-oriented management, an acceptable pay and benefits package, and—especially today—stability.

Many HR professionals advertise nationally, in the belief that someone really great is just waiting for the opportunity to work for the company. Others target national associations, especially for professional and high-level executive positions. A company starting an HR function needs to carefully analyze whether the cost justifies the result. Small and emerging companies usually can find the employees they need locally.

Companies may use search firms for filling top-level or hard-to-fill positions. Sometimes, especially for specialized professional or technical experts and top management with focused experience, this approach can be cost-effective and efficient. However, there are good search firms and poor search firms. Getting assistance and finding consultants are discussed in chapter IX.

Application Forms

Because of the exposure to employee relations litigation and civil rights lawsuits, the application form should not be taken lightly. Some off-the-shelf applications are allegedly validated; however, they may ask for information that, if used in the employment process, would be evidence of discrimination. Although these forms may state that the information should be supplied only if it is job-related, applicants often want the job so much they will supply the information regardless. Later, if a discrimination charge or an employee relations lawsuit is filed, the non-job-related information given by the applicant will be assumed to have been used, and a prima facie case may result.

Other "home-grown" applications may request information about marital status, children, day care arrangements, and past workers' compensation claims. All of this information could be used as evidence of discrimination. Some applications ask for previous names, spouse's name, age of spouse, and number of children. Information that is not specifically job-related should not be requested on an application.

A model application form is included at the end of this chapter (HRII-1.FRM), and SHRM publishes a book of applications that contains many examples for use by all sizes of companies. A company should choose an application that focuses entirely on job-related information required for the initial screening process. Once the number of applicants has been narrowed down to those who meet the minimum qualifications, other information can be requested.

Step 1. Reviewing an Application or Resume

Applications and resumes play different roles in the recruiting and selection process. Traditionally, companies want resumes for professional positions, while standard applications are used for hourly and nonexempt positions. The resume is a marketing tool for the applicant. If written and completed well, it emphasizes the strengths of the applicant for the particular position while minimizing weaknesses and avoiding embarrassing topics or problem areas. Applications provide the information in more rigid form and thus generally can identify gaps in employment history, problem areas, and educational weaknesses. In addition to requesting a resume, it is a good HR practice to require applications even of applicants for professional positions.

Once specific minimum selection criteria have been determined, reviewing both resumes and applications is relatively easy. Remember, the essential job functions must be identified as well as the minimum criteria and the optional characteristics. This process will help focus attention on who should be hired. Keep in mind that the perfect candidate is seldom found.

Reviewing the Cover Letter

Cover letters can provide insight into an applicant's attitudes and abilities to do the job. The questions listed in **Figure II-2** can be used to review cover letters.

Figure II-2. Reviewing the Cover Letter

- Is the letter clean and typed?
- Has it been written in proper business format?
- Is it an original letter specifically tailored to your organization?
- Is it addressed to a specific person in your organization?
- Are the spelling and grammar correct?
- Does the letter achieve its objectives and is it persuasive?

Reviewing the Resume

Although they would deny it, many managers make the mistake of gathering resumes and then reading through for those that have information that catches their attention. Determining the selection criteria and then creating a checklist against which each resume can be compared is a more efficient technique. The questions listed in **Figure II-3** are examples of those that can be used to review a resume.

Generally, a well-researched and well-written resume should get an interview because it suggests a good employee. Conversely, a poorly written resume, despite experience and skills, suggests a poor employee.

Figure II-3. Reviewing the Resume

Overall organization and appearance

- Are there errors in spelling and grammar?
- Did the applicant anticipate a need for the critical data and provide it in the resume?
- Can what the applicant is trying to tell be clearly understood?
- Did the applicant list duties rather than responsibilities?
- Is there a list of significant accomplishments? Be cautious of lists of easily performed tasks or phrases such as "involved in" or "part of."
- How long did the applicant hold each position, and are the titles valid?
- Does the resume show how the experience fits the company's needs? Are the skills and accountabilities transferable?
- Primarily consider only relevant, job-related educational qualifications.
- Does the applicant have too much education for the position?
- Is the applicant interested in this specific position or is it a stepping-stone to another position?
- Although technical requirements may mandate certain courses of study, especially in smaller companies, it is important to be flexible with college degrees.

Other relevant information: This might include college activities, community involvement, awards, church-related activities, hobbies, and participation in sports. Although some of these skills may be relevant to the position being applied for, be careful not to give them too much weight.

Reviewing the Application

If every candidate completes the same application form, it is easier to compare them. Again, as with resumes, the reviewer should have a clear understanding of what the job entails. At this step, be sure to look for the minimum job qualifications, not necessarily the applicant with the most proficiency. (See **Figure II-4**.) Many managers make the mistake of believing that the applicant with the most skills, most experience, or highest level of education is the best candidate. This is seldom true.

Figure II-4. Reviewing the Application

- **Clarity:** How clear are the answers to the questions? Did the applicant rush through the form or take time to do it right? Were the questions answered with relevant information?

- **Legibility:** Can the handwriting be read and does it fit within the lines? Are there a lot of erasures or mistakes? Was care taken to keep the application clean and neat?

- **Experience:** Does the experience offered match the experience required for the job? How is it explained? Can you get a good idea of the person's duties and responsibilities from the description? Does it sound reasonable?

- **Education:** As with experience, check for validity and credibility. Are the courses and degrees consistent with what you are looking for? Only education that is job-related should be considered.

An Application/Resume Evaluation Form **(HRII-2.FRM)** is included at the end of this chapter; it is only an example and should be revised for use by individual companies.

Step 2. Interviewing

Of all the selection methods available, the interview is used most often, yet few managers and hiring agents have the training and skills to conduct interviews effectively and legally. Most interviews rely on gut feelings instead of objective assessments. The typical interview consists of questions about the applicant's work history, education, desires, and skills, but there is much more to interviewing. First, the interviewer should establish that the applicant possesses the basic skills and education. Next, any unclear entries on the resume and application should be discussed. Questions should be asked to determine if the employee is willing to do the work. Finally, the interviewer should attempt to determine how well the employee would fit into the company's culture and work environment.

Procedures for employment interviewing may vary according to the needs of the company and the level of hire.

Manager's Decision

Many companies use a process in which a staff person conducts the prescreening and preliminary selection. The immediate supervisor then interviews (sometimes with other managers or an HR professional) and makes the final decision. This approach usually results in an acceptable employee, but since the decision is made in a vacuum, other people within the organization may not be committed to it.

Team Approach

Many companies have been successful using a team approach in hiring, even with entry-level employees. A team approach is essential for hiring and promoting supervisors and managers; at these levels, it is more important that the person fits into the organization than that the educational and technical qualifications are perfect.

Sometimes all the team members (all members of the work group) participate in the entire selection process, but usually they are only involved in the interviewing process. Each team member makes short presentations on the finalists, identifying the strengths and weaknesses of each. After thorough and open discussion, the candidates are ranked and a finalist is selected. This process may vary depending on the culture of the company.

Panel Choice Approach

In many organizations, those involved in the selection process (HR, the manager, and peers) narrow the applicants down to two or three candidates, and the immediate supervisor chooses one. This approach minimizes the "halo effect," which often clouds the selection process when one candidate stands out early.

The Process

1. Maintain consistency when making hiring decisions. Review the recruitment and selection process and any other considerations such as affirmative action and equal employment opportunity.
2. Be able to document and explain the decision. If you can clearly describe the reasons for the decision, it is likely that good selection practices were used.

During the process, applicants are usually very apprehensive and concerned about when a decision will be made. If the decision does not come quickly, the first choice may take advantage of another opportunity and no longer be available. Many companies tell applicants when they will decide, but there is a concern. When an offer is made, the applicant may want several days to consider all the alternatives. While the company waits for an answer, the other applicants will know that they were not first choice. If the first choice turns down the offer, the second choice may not want the position.

Finally, every applicant who has been interviewed, even through a phone screening, should get a response. If eliminated, the applicant should be notified by letter within a week.

The interviewing process outlined in **Figure II-5** is one many companies use with great success.

Figure II-5. Successful Interviewing

- First, identify the questions that should be asked and write them down. Ask these questions of all applicants.
- Consider the setting; provide a quiet, uninterrupted location that puts the applicant at ease.
- Use discretion in taking notes.
- Observe the applicant's demeanor.
- Let the applicant do the talking.
- Maintain control of the interview and stay within the allocated time.
- Probe incomplete responses.
- Sell the company, but do not oversell the position.
- Close with a positive comment.
- Write an interview summary immediately after the interview.

At the end of this chapter, an Applicant Evaluation Form **(HRII-3.FRM)** has been provided as a model; it can be revised to meet a company's specific needs.

Questions to Avoid Asking

Figure II-6 is based on federal law and general practice; state and local laws may vary. In general, however, federal and state laws and regulations applying to equal employment opportunity prohibit inquiries that express, directly or indirectly, any preference, limitation, specification, or discrimination as to race, religion, color, national origin, sex, age, disability or handicap, marital status, or pregnancy. Check carefully in your state and local area for statutes that may give applicants other rights or limit your discretion in asking questions.

Figure II-6. Interview Questions

Subject	You may ask	You may not ask
Race or color		About complexion or color of skin
Religion or creed		About religious denomination, religious affiliation, church, synagogue, parish, pastor, rabbi, or religious holidays observed.
National origin		About lineage, ancestry, national origin, descent, parentage, nationality, or nationality of parents or spouse.
Sex		No questions or inquiries are permitted.
Marital status		About marital status, living arrangements, spouse's occupation, children, child care arrangements.
Name		Have you changed your name? What is your maiden name? Have you ever worked under another name?
Age	If state child protective and safety laws apply, you may ask if the applicant is over that minimum age.	No other questions or inquiries are permitted. (Certain public sector occupations may have bona fide age requirements.)
Disability/handicap	Here are the job requirements of the position. Is there any reason that you cannot perform all the activities of the job?	Do you have a disability? Have you filed any workers' compensation claims? Have you been treated for any of the following diseases? Have you had recent or past surgeries or past medical problems?
Birthplace		About birthplace; birthplace of spouse, parents, or other relatives.

Subject	You may ask	You may not ask
Photograph		An applicant may not be asked to affix a photograph to an application or a resume at any time before actual employment.
Citizenship	Do you have the legal right to work in the United States and do you have documenation of that right?	Are you a U.S. citizen? In what country do you have citizenship? Are you a naturalized U.S. citizen? When did you become a citizen?
Criminal history	Were you ever convicted of a felony? *(This question can be asked only if the inquiry is job-related and there is a significant business necessity.)*	Were you ever arrested? If so, when, where, and what was the disposition? How many traffic tickets have you received?
Language	What foreign languages do you read fluently? Write fluently? Speak fluently? Do you speak and write English fluently? (Only if job-related.)	How did you learn to speak (foreign language)? Do you speak (foreign language) at home? How did you acquire the ability to speak (foreign language)?
Education	About academic, vocational, or professional education or public or private schools attended.	Did your parents pay for your education? Did they help you pay for your education? Are your parents college graduates? When did you attend college? (Dates may provide information about applicant's age.)
Experience	About applicant's work history, experience, strengths, and weaknesses.	
Relatives	Do you have any relatives employed by this company?	Names, addresses, ages, number or other information concerning children or other relatives not employed by the company.
Military experience	(This area is not clear because some case law has found that using military service or type of discharge may have a disparate impact upon minority servicemen. It is advisable to use military service as work experience.)	General questions about the applicant's military experience.
Organizations	Are you a member of any professional organization that is relevant to the position for which you are applying?	About the clubs, societies, and organizations of which the applicant is a member.

Sample Interview Questions

Management Position

1. **How would you define the job of a manager?** Generally, you want to find out how the individual sees the position of management. The description should match the style and personality prevalent in your company.

2. **Do your subordinates report directly and solely to you or on a project basis?** The ruination of a good managerial candidate often starts with the interviewer's belief that all managers achieve success using the same methods. Many managers today see their role as more of a leader, facilitator, and team builder than as someone who gives all the orders. Some managers are traditional in their approach, but delegate extensively. Because of company culture, most managers continue to focus on short-term objectives and many try to control every detail of their subordinates' work. Selecting a top-down traditional applicant for a position in a company that is democratic in its management style will result in problems for both the employee and the company.

3. **Have you had more terminations or voluntary resignations in your career?** If the applicant has had quite a few jobs, the interviewer needs to explore the circumstances of the changes.

4. **How would you interview applicants?** Watch out for applicants who take this question casually or say they are experienced enough to recognize a good applicant.

5. **What steps do you normally take to get a new employee up to speed?** The great majority of managers believe that training and orientation are important to the success of new employees. Ask for examples. Beware of the applicant who says he or she hires only fully qualified employees, and that they shouldn't need training.

6. **How do you maintain discipline in your department?** What special problems does the candidate have with day-to-day management of staff?

7. **What is your philosophy of management?** The successful candidate has a philosophy of management congruent with that of his or her new manager. This shared vision will enhance their ability to communicate effectively with each other and support each other's values.

Clerical Position

1. **Where do you see yourself six months, a year, or two years from now?** With the ever-changing workforce, a company is looking for someone who sees the position as a career rather than just a job; this difference might distinguish a hard worker from a clock watcher. But if the company culture is "my way or the highway," the interviewer might want to explore opportunities with someone who just wants a job, not an opportunity to grow or to be creative.

2. **Tell me about a time when you went about a task in your own way rather than following instructions.** The answers to these questions can give a good picture of how the applicant views taking initiative versus following instructions. If the company wants to avoid hiring people who do as they please, the interviewer might want to ask some follow-up questions. But if the company wants someone who takes initiative, the person who cannot function without direction from the boss is going to be a failure.

Recent College Graduates

1. **How do you think your grades should be considered by your first employer?** Look for someone who can back up her or his answers with sound reasoning. Someone who thinks he or she doesn't have anything else to learn may be a management problem.

2. **What job in our company would you choose if you were free to do so?** What would the candidate like to be doing in two years? Five years? These probes help identify signs of direction, inner strength, ambition, and confidence. Follow up by asking, "Why would you want that job?"

Step 3. Reference and Background Checks

Reference, Credential, and Credit Checks

The application form should include a section that gives the company permission to check job references. If a resume is used, the applicant should be asked to sign a separate statement giving this permission.

Reference and background checks play a crucial role in the selection process. Under general tort theory, employers may face litigation for the negligent hiring and retention of employees who engage in misconduct both during and after working hours. The theory is that employers have a duty to protect workers, customers, and visitors from injury caused by employees who the employer knew (or should have known) posed a risk. This obligation exists even if the injury occurs miles away from the worksite.

Former employers are usually reluctant to provide information beyond employment dates, job titles, and ending salary. They usually praise the employee. As of this writing, eight states have passed legislation providing a qualified privilege to former employers who, in good faith, give job references based on fact. This legislation might make it easier to get valid references.

The following are some successful techniques used by recruiting and search firms to obtain references when the former employer has policies against providing more than the minimum information.

- If you call the employee's department and are referred to human resources, try the department again. Someone else may give more accurate information. (Note: If a company wants to protect itself, it will avoid allowing anyone—especially line supervisors—except trained staff to give company references.)
- Contact someone who has worked with the applicant. Everyone likes to talk and you may gather valuable information.
- Call the personal references listed on the application and ask probing questions. People often give very valuable information after the caller has developed rapport with them.
- Always ask for job-related information to avoid collecting non-job-related information that may provide the basis for a discrimination charge.

With some planning and sufficient time, anyone can be successful in checking references. A Request for Reference Form **(HRII-4.FRM)** is included at the end of this chapter.

Educational Credentials

It is not uncommon for applicants to exaggerate their education credentials. Although many companies check credentials for professional and management positions, the company needs to make a value judgment on whether it is worth the time and effort. The longer an applicant has been in the workforce, the less relevant his or her education may be as a qualification for the position. Most educational institutions will release graduation information only at the written request of the applicant. If the company decides to check education accomplishments, it should make sure the query includes all relevant information, including degrees earned.

Fair Credit Reporting Act (1970)

Many employers feel the need to check credit history. The Fair Credit Reporting Act requires employers to inform applicants in writing that an inquiry into the applicant's financial status will be conducted. Applicants must be informed if they are denied employment because of information obtained during the inquiry and must be given the name and address of the third party who investigated them.

Employers should be careful in conducting credit checks. These checks must be in response to valid job-related requirements. Blanket credit checks of all employees might be found illegal if they are not job-related, especially if the results show an adverse impact on minorities or females.

Background Checks

Many companies use agencies to conduct background checks of applicants. Except for very high level management positions, the cost usually doesn't justify the results. In addition, the input form used by these agencies often asks for information that could be considered evidence of discrimination or a violation of

ADA. An application/input form from one of these companies, sold nationally, is poorly designed and written. The form asks for background checks for credit history and criminal history and includes a request for information about an applicant's history of reporting workers' compensation claims. The ADA prohibits such information from being used in the selection process. Even if it is not used, having it in an employee's personnel file or in the file of an applicant who was not hired gives the impression that information was used.

Consider carefully any decision to use background checks as part of an employment screening process. Seek advice from knowledgeable human resource practitioners, consultants, or employee relations lawyers.

Step 4. Physical Examinations and Testing

Testing as a selection method is popular with managers and HR professionals. The business community likes to include physical and psychological screening among its hiring tools. Whatever the reason a company decides to test, a clearly defined policy and a comprehensive plan need to be developed. Inconsistent application of the policy alienates applicants and employees and opens the company to possible litigation and fines.

Before considering testing, the company should get advice and direction from knowledgeable human resource practitioners, consultants, or employee relations lawyers.

Preemployment Physical Examinations

Since the enactment of ADA, it has been unlawful to require an applicant to submit to a physical examination until after a conditional offer of employment has been made. The company is required to make "reasonable accommodation" for the applicant's disability unless it would cause an "undue business hardship." As a practical matter, very few disabilities cannot be accommodated with a reasonable expense.

Post-offer physical examinations are lawful and can be very useful. An applicant with a disability that cannot be accommodated does not have to be hired. Physical examinations can identify preexisting work-related disabilities that in most states are subject to the "second injury fund." And a preemployment physical examination can be used as evidence of preexisting health problems (for example, hearing loss) for which the employer will not be liable.

Drug and Alcohol Testing

For the most part, employers are not required to conduct drug screens, except for those involved in commercial transportation and subject to Department of Transportation regulations and government contractors who are subject to the Drug-Free Workplace Act. State laws may govern drug and alcohol testing—be sure to check with the appropriate state office. Drug and alcohol testing can be legally conducted before a conditional offer of employment; however, most employers using both drug screening and physical examinations combine the two and conduct them after a conditional offer of employment.

If a company chooses to conduct drug screening, it must notify applicants and employees of its intention. If company management does not see the value of screening or is not committed to it, it should avoid conducting the tests. The courts have generally upheld the legality of preemployment drug and alcohol testing. Less clear but also generally upheld is mandatory testing for cause, especially as part of safety and accident prevention programs. The practice of random testing is the one most open to questions and objections from employees. Before considering drug and alcohol screening, the company should get advice from knowledgeable human resource practitioners, consultants, or employee relations lawyers; develop a comprehensive plan; and discuss the process with employees.

Honesty Screening

The Employee Polygraph Protection Act (1988) was passed in response to abuses by employers using the polygraph both for employment screening and to determine the honesty of employees. The act restricts most employers from using lie detector tests without reasonable suspicion of workplace theft or other misconduct. The act recognizes that such tests are unreliable and often inaccurate.

In response, employers began using pen-and-pencil "honesty" tests in which applicants or employees write responses and make signed statements about their behaviors and values. Accuracy has been the main controversy—these examinations have been found unreliable and inaccurate. The test developers and publishers contend that there is a correlation between test findings and performance on the job and personal honesty; however, the courts have routinely discounted the relationship and ruled against companies that use them.

One major test publisher routinely advertises that its written instrument is or has been validated by the EEOC. The Uniform Selection Guidelines require that each instrument a company uses be validated for use in that particular company. An instrument used by one company with no adverse impact may have an adverse impact in another company, even if it is used on a similar workforce applicant base. If the use of some selection device results in an adverse impact, the company may not use the instrument unless no other selection processes are available.

A company using these instruments should consider carefully and seek professional human resource advice. The exposure to employee relations liability is significant. For further information, consult the reading list in appendix A.

Handwriting Analysis

Handwriting analysis is mentioned briefly because it has been popular in Europe and is slowly gaining acceptance in the United States. It involves a review of the physical characteristics of an applicant's handwriting compared with that of other individuals. As with other pen-and-pencil instruments, the courts have found little evidence of a correlation between results of the analysis and job performance or honesty.

Skills and Aptitude Testing

These tests measure the applicant's ability to do a task or use a skill. They usually involve a combination of written tests and demonstrations of ability. Although these tests can predict job performance, many have an adverse impact on females and minorities, which may make them illegal under the provisions of the Uniform Selection Guidelines.

Step 5. Making the Hiring Decision

Many studies show managers do not do a very good job of hiring. It is a commonly accepted fact that if the applicant makes a poor impression in the first five minutes, there is an 80 percent chance he or she will not be considered further. Another survey found that in more than 30 percent of selections, the last person interviewed was the one hired. Still another study suggests that in more than 80 percent of selection decisions, an employee is chosen who projects the same image as the manager or the former employee. Many employers go with their gut feeling when making hiring decisions. Even with professional human resource advice, poor hiring decisions are often made.

There are ways to make a prudent and successful decision and avoid poor hires. If the recommendations made so far have been followed, the essential data are available.

- The position has been analyzed and the essential functions identified. Both required and desired characteristics have been listed.
- The prescreening process identified candidates who meet the essential qualifications of the position.
- Interviews of applicants who passed the first cut distinguished between those who were not suitable, those who were acceptable, and those who were extremely qualified. A second round of interviews may have been scheduled for those who were extremely qualified.
- Of those who were extremely qualified, experience, education, and job history were verified. Any other selection devices, such as written tests or psychological profiles, were conducted. None of this group of candidates should be eliminated at this step.
- The manager should have enlisted the help of his or her peers to prepare a list on which applicants were ranked according to the data gathered and the evaluators' perceptions.

The top applicant on the ranked list should receive a conditional offer of employment. Any salary negotiation should take place at this step. The applicant should be given no more than a few days to consider the offer. If the applicant accepts, a physical should be scheduled. If the applicant declines, the next-ranked applicant should be offered the job. This process continues until a selection is made. (Note: Second-, third-, and fourth-choice applicants should not be notified of their rejection until an offer of employment has been accepted by the top applicant. The manager should be prepared to offer the position to the next-ranked applicant, since the differences among the top applicants will be small.)

All applicants should be sent a letter notifying them that the position has been filled.

Companies that are successful and competitive evaluate the quality of their product or service. One of the most important factors in the success of any company is its employees, yet few companies evaluate the effectiveness of the recruiting and selection procedures they use and focus on improving them.

Step 6. New Employee Orientation

The essence of effective management is to get the job done right through other people. The degree of success in reaching this goal will depend on the quality of performance that managers get from their employees. Performance hinges upon how efficiently and conscientiously employees respond to the instructions they receive, the standards the organization sets for them, and the company culture and rules under which they function.

The work environment and the performance and behavior that an employee establishes during the first few weeks of employment will have a strong influence on that employee's attitude, productivity, and team spirit for months and years to come.

A former personnel manager and mentor taught me a valuable lesson: Once bad habits and unacceptable standards of performance are developed, they are hard to change. Employees tend to fall into good or bad patterns early in their employment. Steering new employees along desirable paths is a primary responsibility of management. It is generally left to the human resource staff to advise managers how best to accomplish this objective and how to monitor success.

What can be done to better prepare new employees for the work environment? They should be informed that they are expected to perform to their maximum, and they should be managed so that conflicts are resolved satisfactorily. If it is necessary to terminate an employee, the workplace environment must support the belief that "if someone is let go here, it must be deserved."

In most organizations, the orientation process is short. It focuses primarily on filling out personnel forms, reading the job description, reviewing the company handbook, taking a tour of the new surroundings, meeting co-workers, and getting the workstation ready. All of these activities are important, but the best way to cultivate a positive, committed, high-performance employee is through an introduction to the values, culture, and expected work ethic. With the high cost of hiring a new employee and the substantial cost of turnover, companies can no longer afford to lose this chance. They can no longer treat the employee orientation process casually.

Creating an efficient and successful orientation process takes time and effort. Before starting to develop a new employee orientation, you might want to get the opinions of those who have recently joined your company. You also might want to use the task committee approach, in which you invite both new hires and veterans to participate in the development. The following are some guidelines and suggestions for topics and activities to include in an orientation.

Planning for Orientation

1. What information will employees need to feel comfortable in their new surroundings?
2. What impressions should be made on the first day? (What impressions would I like to receive if I were the new employee?)
3. What key policies and procedures must the employee be made aware of the first day so that mistakes will not be made on the second day? (Stick to vital issues.)
4. What can I do to ensure that the person will begin to know his or her fellow employees without feeling overwhelmed?
5. What can I do to make the person feel physically comfortable, welcome, and secure (desk, work area, etc.)?
6. What tasks can I teach the person to do on the first day to provide a sense of accomplishment?
7. What positive experience can I provide for the new employee that he or she can talk about at home?
8. How can I ensure that I will be available on the new employee's first day to convey a clear message that he or she is an important addition to the team?

The First Week

1. Sketch a brief overview of the organization's structure.
2. Explain, in general terms, the organization's objectives and values. Provide a written statement of both.
3. Conduct a general item-by-item review of key policies and procedures.
4. Explain the fringe benefits that will affect the employee, and provide any written material on those benefits.
5. Present general information on personnel growth and training opportunities available through the organization, and information on promotional opportunities.
6. Provide details on work safety and schedule training if safety is an issue in your organization.
7. Specify the general parameters of the new employee's job, especially as it relates to other people and their jobs.
8. Review the new employee's job description, including the scope of authority and how this can be increased.
9. Introduce special policies and procedures of the department or supervisor.
10. Explain evaluation standards and procedures.
11. Detail probationary and disciplinary procedures.
12. Provide information on special forms, reference materials, and other details the employee needs to know.

30-Day Checkpoints

As the first month progresses, new employees should settle into a productive pattern of job performance and should begin to focus on their long-term relationship with the organization. If planning and training have been adequate, new employees should be generating enough work to be evaluated. Objective feedback at this stage can have a considerable impact on new employees' perceptions of themselves and of the job. In evaluating employees, remember these five points:

1. Use standards that are realistic, clear, and objective, and that were explained to the new employee at orientation.
2. Assess the performance, not the person.
3. Be as descriptive (rather than evaluative) as possible.
4. Be sure that appraisal comments relate directly to standards.
5. After presenting data, listen carefully and do not dismiss or discount the employee's comments—you may learn a great deal.

There is a time to be lenient and a time to be flexible. It is important to make the point to new employees at the outset of their employment that rules and standards must be adhered to. To encourage the development of a loyal, committed, long-term employee, the company must communicate effectively and forcefully that breaches of rules and standards will not be tolerated.

HRII-1.FRM

An Equal Employment Opportunity Employer

Notice to applicant: We appreciate your interest in the company and assure you we are interested in your qualifications. A clear understanding of your background and work history will aid us in placing you in the position that best meets your qualifications and may assist us in future upgrading. It is to your advantage to give complete and detailed answers to the questions in this application.

1. The company does not discriminate in its employment practices on the basis of race, color, religion, sex, national origin, age, or disabilities. Questions on this application relating to such characteristics will be used for government reporting purposes.

2. Many positions with the company, including secretarial and clerical positions, require some physical ability and the ability to lift moderate weights. Please consider this. We will make reasonable accommodations in altering the requirements of the position when possible. However, because of the nature of our services and business necessity, we are limited in what we can do.

3. The company has an extensive nonsmoking policy that prohibits smoking while at work, during working hours, or while providing services for the company and/or its clients. Applicants who smoke may want to inquire about the policy before completing this application.

Name: (last)   (first)   (middle—spell out)

Address: (street)   (city/state)   (zip)

Telephone number where you can be reached between 8:30 a.m. and 4:30 p.m.:

Positions desired:

1.   2.   3.   4.

Circle status desired: Full-time   Part-time   Temporary

Do you authorize inquiry from your present employer?   Yes   No

Do you authorize inquiry from your previous employers?   Yes   No

Do you have the legal right to work in the United States?   Yes   No

Does anything restrict your ability to perform all the functions of the job you are applying for? If yes, please explain.   Yes   No

HRII-1.FRM (p. 2)

List employment beginning with your present or last position. Request additional sheets if necessary.

DATES:	EMPLOYERS:	DUTIES:
From (mo. & yr.):	Name:	Job title:
To (mo. & yr.):	Address:	Principal duties:
Hours per week:	City & state:	
Final salary:	Supervisor/phone#:	Reason for leaving:
From (mo. & yr.):	Name:	Job title:
To (mo. & yr.):	Address:	Principal duties:
Hours per week:	City & state:	
Final salary:	Supervisor/phone#:	Reason for leaving:
From (mo. & yr.):	Name:	Job title:
To (mo. & yr.):	Address:	Principal duties:
Hours per week:	City & state:	
Final salary:	Supervisor/phone#:	Reason for leaving:
From (mo. & yr.):	Name:	Job title:
To (mo. & yr.):	Address:	Principal duties:
Hours per week:	City & state:	
Final salary:	Supervisor/phone# :	Reason for leaving:

PLEASE READ THE FOLLOWING STATEMENT CAREFULLY BEFORE SIGNING THIS APPLICATION

In filling out this application, I understand the company is in no way obligated to provide employment nor am I obligated to accept employment. I understand my application will remain active for consideration for six months. I understand past employment records and other facts stated by me may be subject to inquiry. I hereby grant the company permission to check any of this information. I understand that my acceptance for employment is contingent upon satisfactorily passing a physical examination that will include a drug screen. I further understand any misrepresentation or omission of facts in this application will be sufficient cause for cancellation and/or separation if I have been employed.

Signature: _____   Date : _____

HRII-2.FRM

Application/Resume Evaluation Form

Applicant's Name	Total Rating	Organization	Experience	Education	Other Activities

HRII-3.FRM

Applicant Evaluation Form

Applicant's name: _____

Date: _____   Time: _____

Weight	Rating	Essential Requirements	How Demonstrated

Weight	Rating	Desired Requirements	

Comments:

HRII-4.FRM

Request for Reference Form

To:

Date: _____

Name: _____   Social Security number: _____

has applied to us for employment as a _____ and has stated that he/she was

in your employ from _____ to _____ in the capacity of _____ .

Please complete the following form and return it to us in the self-addressed envelope at your earliest convenience.

Signed: _____

Director of Human Resources

Date of employment: _____   Date of termination: _____

Position(s) held: _____   Ending salary: _____

_____

_____

Comments: _____

_____

_____

_____

_____

CHAPTER III

PERFORMANCE IMPROVEMENT STRATEGIES

A common problem companies have in starting an HR function is performance appraisals. Developing a process for a workforce composed of employees with different personalities, attitudes, and aptitudes is not an easy task. The most important responsibility of managers is to evaluate effectiveness, reward performance that meets expectations, and correct performance that does not. Many managers put off giving performance reviews; sometimes it is because they do not like to criticize employees or they do not know how to evaluate performance objectively. Usually, appraisals do not result in corrected behavior.

Employees want to know how they are doing and be recognized for good performance. Discrimination charges are multiplying, and there are increased opportunities for a disgruntled or frustrated employee to use the courts to resolve employee relations problems. It is crucial that managers learn the techniques required to conduct effective performance appraisals.

Managers who correct poor performance objectively and fire when necessary avoid costly discrimination charges and employee relations lawsuits. The company will have a more committed and dedicated workforce with more employee stability and less turnover. A company starting an HR function has a great opportunity to prove the value of human resource management and its effect on company profitability.

This chapter is divided into two parts. First, performance appraisals, both informal and formal, are discussed, including setting performance goals, conducting appraisals, agreeing on corrective action, and documenting the conversation. In the second part of the chapter, suggestions are given on changing behaviors through formal corrective action and discipline, and on how to fire employees and stay out of court.

Performance Appraisals

The Changing Environment

Most employees have experienced the highs and lows of good and not so good ratings. In addition to inaccurate ratings, the clumsy and unprofessional manner in which some managers conduct the formal part of the process causes problems. Many business consultants and writers chide managers for the poor quality and misguided use of performance appraisals. The situation is so bad that many managers are tempted to abolish the annual performance appraisal and the linking of performance ratings to pay increases.

However, performance appraisals are one of the most valuable and important tools available to management. Successful companies require measurement to value profitability, manage costs, ensure safety and accident prevention, staff the company correctly, conserve resources, improve marketing and sales, conduct research, and develop products. In most companies, the performance appraisal is the main strategy for motivating and retaining valued employees and the primary vehicle for awarding compensation and pay increases.

If performance appraisals are so valuable, why are there so many obstacles? Is too much emphasis placed on the process? Is the process used to accomplish the wrong objectives? Are companies using unfair, highly subjective standards? Do employees believe that each has to be number one and that being average or being rated satisfactory is not acceptable?

As global competition confronts U.S. business, companies are increasingly under pressure to more fully use the workforce, to get more done with fewer people. Some managers believe current performance appraisals are barriers to positive employee relations, efficiency, and productivity. Many have discarded the practice altogether in favor of team-based evaluations and bonuses based on organizational success. Some top companies follow the teaching of W. Edwards Deming and question the value of the annual performance appraisal. Scrutinizing how the process actually is conducted, there is evidence that annual performance appraisals are poorly handled and that the process does not increase value-added activity. Other evidence suggests that the process is often a subterfuge for backing into a pay raise.

However, prevailing company thinking supports continuing annual individual performance appraisals. Even consultants working with total quality management (TQM) do not advocate discarding appraisals. Besides legal concerns, there are other job-related reasons for conducting them. With laws prohibiting discrimination in all personnel processes, promotions, pay increases, and performance must be based on job performance measurements. Maintaining valid records of employees' performance is crucial.

The Appraisal Process

A model performance evaluation and corrective action process is shown in **Figure III-1**.

The crucial part of the performance appraisal process is not rating the employee; it is the employee's reaction to the assessment. This is where lawsuits are won and lost. This is where most managers provoke hostile responses from employees even while trying to convey favorable evaluations. Discussing performance has the potential to disrupt even the best working relationship and to evoke emotional responses. The way managers conduct appraisals has been criticized as irrelevant, self-serving, and futile. Employees become frustrated and disheartened, lose their commitment, and generally become ineffective. Substantial evidence exists that setting goals together can increase achievement. Managers should encourage employee participation in setting goals and agreed-upon measures of job performance.

Benefits of a Well-Planned Appraisal

When managers see the appraisal process as on ongoing management responsibility, it becomes possible to help employees develop the skills they lack. When feedback is consistently given, problems are solved as they arise. A good performance appraisal has the characteristics identified in **Figure III-2**.

The Setting

The effective performance appraisal is a job-related planning activity shared by the employee and the supervisor. Input from both is essential for a successful outcome. The performance appraisal process can pro-

Figure III-1. Performance Appraisal and Corrective Action

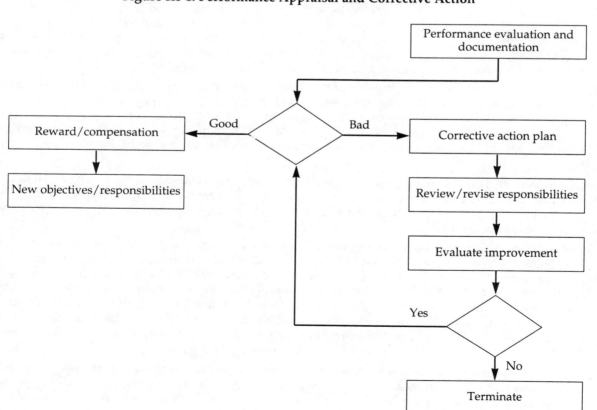

Figure III-2. Characteristics of a Good Performance Appraisal System

- Identifies performance goals.
- Aids in selection and recruiting.
- Provides feedback.
- Includes training and development.
- Facilitates promotion and, if appropriate, transfer.
- Rewards and recognizes achievement.
- Formalizes and documents goals and specific activities.
- Predicts performance on present and future jobs.
- Identifies areas where performance is good and where it can be improved.
- Identifies specific areas of improvement and the process required.
- Documents broader opportunities and career development.
- Links achievement and compensation.

vide both the appraiser and the employee with a sense of accomplishment, direction in priorities, and commitment to a specific career path.

Employees need to know how they have been rated. They need a clear understanding of how they fared in the eyes of their appraiser and their organization. The interview gives the appraiser an opportunity to discuss the rating, the rationale, and future development.

To emphasize the importance of the meeting, the appraiser and the employee should conduct the interview in an environment that is private and comfortable, where they will not be interrupted or distracted.

The Form

No part of the performance appraisal process has received more attention than the design of the rating instrument. To many managers, the performance appraisal process is nothing more than the sheet of paper that documents the performance. The form is more important than the process and the results. Consultants see an almost bizarre interest in the design of the form and little else. Managers search for that one basic document that can be used to rate all employees in the organization.

Over the years, a variety of forms and instruments have been designed to help managers rate and document employee performance. The passage of the Civil Rights Act of 1964 characterized performance appraisal forms as a test of adverse impact. Courts found that performance standards were often arbitrary and not job-related, and that some commonly used forms seemed to discriminate. Companies try to focus attention on performance measurements and the communication process, but forms are important as guidelines to managers and as documentation.

Most appraisal forms today include (1) a narrative descriptive review, (2) a checklist of job-related responsibilities and duties, (3) performance dimensions and rating scales, and (4) goal setting and results achieved. However, no matter how valid and accurate a form may be, poor judgment often makes the appraisal invalid. The most simple instrument uses a set of rating scales on which to rate many measurements or characteristics of expected performance. Other procedures commonly used include forced-choice and mixed-standard rating systems. Some performance appraisal instruments include a management by objectives (MBO) approach or a combination of MBO and forced choice. Several companies use a process of identifying key objectives and then describing the performance in narrative form.

Some model instruments are included at the end of this chapter to provide a foundation for discussing the essential components of any appraisal form. They are not intended to be used without modification for a specific company.

Before designing an appraisal form, the company may want to discuss the questions in **Figure III-3**.

Figure III-3. Designing a Performance Appraisal Form

- What information does the company need from the appraisal process?
- What does the company want to measure?
- What degree of validity and reliability does the company need?
- What degree of validity and reliability is possible with the management in the organization?
- Should specific procedures and instruments be designed for specific work units and levels (e.g., exempt versus nonexempt) within the company?
- What adverse or undesired effect may occur because of the use of the specific rating procedure or form?
- Should the performance appraisal instrument be developed in-house or should outside consultants be used?
- What kinds of checks and balances should be used to ensure rater reliability?
- Is the benefit worth the cost?

Simple ranking

A simple performance appraisal process is to have managers rank individual employees against specified job-related performance standards and then rank order all employees. This method is usually used with some form of normal distribution or bell curve. Although some would object to the subjective nature of this process, it can be accurate and valid, especially in small companies where the raters know each member of the work group well, know the job requirements, and can suppress personal biases. However, a major problem is usually the inability to justify the ratings, especially to those ranked in the lower half of the group. This problem is especially significant in light of research that indicates that nearly all employees believe themselves to be above average.

Narrative descriptive review procedures

These procedures include the essay form and the critical incident form, each of which requires the manager to write a description of the employee's performance. Ordinarily some specific rating is included that the manager must assign to the performance. Many consultants avoid this type of review procedure; however, these techniques have been used efficiently and productively, especially in smaller companies. The following are brief descriptions.

Essay method. The manager describes the employee within broad categories. These might include an overall impression of the employee's performance, the jobs the employee currently can and cannot do, the strengths and weaknesses of the employee, and the employee's readiness for promotion. This method can be extremely useful in describing performance that managers cannot identify in the more structured checklist format.

Critical incident technique. The manager maintains a log containing observations of successful and unsuccessful performance. Although this method requires close supervision and observation, documentation is easy. The technique is often used in companies where an employee may work for many supervisors, such as shift workers in manufacturing. A serious weakness is the elapsed time between the incident and the formal appraisal. The competence of the manager also influences whether the descriptions are straightforward, honest, and accurate.

The checklist. Checklists use a list of job requirements, behaviors, and traits. The manager reviews the checklist and values the performance of the employee as to the particular behavior or trait. Some checklists assign a weight to each item to permit a more accurate score. Some companies use a more sophisticated checklist to reduce bias and the ability of the manager to inflate the evaluation of the performance.

Goal Setting

Setting individual goals and management by objectives are very popular. In these MBO techniques, the employee works toward a goal that usually has been agreed upon with the manager. The goal becomes the standard that will be used to measure results achieved or behavior modified. There are two weaknesses in these techniques. First, setting measurable goals is difficult for certain positions. Second, managers often set easy-to-attain goals that inflate job parameters and rated performance. This situation occurs when managers try to link the performance rating to a pay increase. **Figure III-4** identifies some critical issues to consider.

Figure III-4. Critical Issues in Management by Objectives

- Goals may be unachievable or too easy to achieve.
- Goals do not measure performance that adds value to the bottom line.
- Managers and employees are not trained.
- Employees may give equal priority to each objective rather than prioritizing.
- It is difficult to compare the success of one individual to that of another.

Rating Scales

Although many managers would like to use the performance appraisal instrument as a definitive measure of an employee's performance and value to the organization, there are limits to describing and appraising human performance. Performance appraisals will never be completely objective. In trying to develop useful measures, a rating scale is often the best device. Rating scales are easy to administer, transfer to quantitative terms, permit standardization, and relate to levels of performance dimensions.

There are problems, however, in defining the various descriptions and applying them to the employee's behavior. Although it is usually easy to differentiate between the top 20 percent and bottom 20 percent, it is very difficult to differentiate among the middle 60 percent. Finally, it is easy for a manager, wishing to exaggerate the performance rating, to give a fake or false reading.

A simple adjective rating scale is common in companies, using descriptors such as *unsatisfactory, marginal, satisfactory, commendable,* and *superior.* Some companies try to get away from the "only satisfactory" category by using descriptors such as *does not meet expectations, meets expectations,* and *exceeds expectations.*

Behaviorally anchored rating scales (BARS) are descriptions of various degrees of behavior with regard to a specific performance level. BARS are usually constructed by identifying the behaviors normally present in a particular job and then separating those required to be successful from those that would result in unsatisfactory or unacceptable performance.

Choosing the Best Approach

A company starting a performance appraisal process should look for the simplest tool possible. A complicated process will take too much time and effort and may be misused.

There are many possible combinations of methods and techniques for performance appraisal. Companies should use caution when considering the use of preprinted forms from the office supply store or a form used by another company, no matter how well designed. Consultants who conduct human resource assessments regularly find errors or requests for information that could lead to charges of unequal treatment or discrimination.

The forms at the end of this chapter are examples of what some companies use. They are not offered for use "as is"; rather, a company should go through the data analysis and assessment process and develop an appraisal form or instrument that meets its own specific needs.

Although most appraisal forms and instruments can be used for all levels of employees, companies may use different forms for hourly, nonexempt, and exempt employees. The hourly and nonexempt appraisal forms are less sophisticated and easier to complete. The exempt appraisal forms are usually a little more extensive and precise because the employees have broader responsibilities and accountabilities. Top executives are seldom appraised using standard instruments. If a formal process is used at all, it is a written narrative.

The Performance Appraisal Form—Nonexempt **(HRIII-1.FRM)** is a checklist combined with a brief narrative. The form forces the manager to rate the employee on five aspects of performance that the company has identified as contributing to employee success. The number of aspects evaluated can be increased or decreased. This form does not quantify the five aspects, and the overall rating may or may not be the sum of the five ratings.

Performance Appraisal Form (A) **(HRIII-2.FRM)** for exempt employees can be adapted for use with nonexempt employees (especially those in technical jobs) if a detailed form is necessary. This form uses a checklist, a brief narrative, and goal setting to provide a very detailed view of an employee's performance. The seven aspects of performance include descriptive phrases that provide direction to the manager and limit the opportunity for inflating the performance rating. At the end of the form, the manager and the employee review objectives from the previous 12 months and set objectives for the next year. The form does not use numerical scores for performance. An overall rating is given, which may or may not be the sum of all ratings and success in meeting objectives. Again, managers should focus more on obtaining mutual agreement on performance and less on the ratings per se.

Performance Appraisal Form (B)—Exempt **(HRIII-3.FRM)** focuses primarily on a narrative description of performance. The form is four pages long and provides much more space for the manager to describe performance. It requires the manager to answer several questions regarding continuous improvement and gives little opportunity for negative or critical comments. This form also provides an opportunity for employee comments. These comments are for purposes of documentation only; if the manager has completed the appraisal process correctly, there should be no reason for rebuttal.

Finally, the Annual Performance Expectations Form **(HRIII-4.FRM)** was designed for a company that wanted to incorporate a brief MBO form into its performance appraisal process. This form allowed them to document objectives without complicating the performance appraisal process.

Guidelines for Useful Feedback

Feedback is a way of helping people consider changing their behavior. It tells a person how his or her actions affect others, based on overall company objectives. Feedback helps individuals keep their behavior on target and thus better achieve their goals. It is a key tool in the performance appraisal process, yet managers routinely fail to obtain the maximum benefit because they often do not listen. How can managers improve their ability to give and receive feedback? In giving feedback, both giver and receiver should check with each other on the accuracy of the communications. See **Figure III-5** for some tips on giving feedback.

Figure III-5. Tips on Giving Feedback

- It should be descriptive rather than evaluative. Avoiding evaluative language reduces the need for the individual to respond defensively.

- It should be specific rather than general. To be told that one is "dominating" will probably not be as useful as to be told, "You did not listen to what others said, and I felt forced to accept your arguments or face attack from you."

- It should take into account the needs of both the receiver and giver. Feedback can be destructive when it serves only the manager's needs.

- It should be directed toward behavior about which the receiver can do something.

- It should be solicited rather than imposed. Feedback is useful when the receiver has asked for it and less so if it is not asked for.

- It should be well-timed.

- It should be checked to ensure the communication is clear and was received the way it was meant.

Corrective Action

Few organizations escape the need to correct the behavior of employees, yet managers in most organizations avoid disciplining employees rather than confronting them. Experience does not prepare most supervisors to administer discipline—when faced with the need to discipline an employee, they are at a loss. The principal elements of a good employee corrective action program are identified in **Figure III-6**.

Figure III-6. Corrective Action

- **Standards:** Standards for performance and appropriate behavior should be established and clearly communicated to all employees.
- **Facts:** The burden is on the supervisor to establish the facts upon which the decision was based.
- **Consistency:** When managers discipline consistently, they gain the support and respect of their employees.
- **Timeliness:** Discipline should follow as soon as possible after the specific behavior that warrants correction.
- **Appropriate discipline:** The discipline imposed should be appropriate for the circumstances and the employee's behavior.
- **Positive action:** If discipline is corrective and positive, a change of behavior is more likely to result.
- **Realistic expectations:** If discipline will not produce or has not produced a change in behavior, the employee should be removed for the benefit of all.

Application of these basic principles will benefit both the employee and the supervisor. The employee will be clear on the standard of behavior required and the consequences that will follow from not meeting that standard. Supervisors are more comfortable when employees perform satisfactorily and behave appropriately.

Dealing with Problem Employees

There are many sources of inappropriate employee behavior. Supervisors are responsible for eliminating these behaviors regardless of the source. When the cause of the inappropriate behavior is the employee's personal life, the supervisor can help the employee recognize his or her responsibility to change the behavior and the need to confront and work through the problems.

Employees can solve their own problems and change their inappropriate behavior; however, they may need help in distinguishing among behavior, feelings, and opinions. The supervisor can be a sounding board for ideas, encourage straight thinking, give assurance that improvement is possible, and help by following a problem through to a successful solution. While the employee ultimately must correct his or her own actions, the supervisor can be a powerful factor in that process.

Sometimes, for various reasons, the employee insists upon being difficult, creates friction in the work group, and blocks productivity. Actions such as these are likely to stir up emotional reactions that may cloud the supervisor's judgment. At this point, the supervisor should consider the questions identified in **Figure III-7**.

Figure III-7. Corrective Action for Supervisors

- Have I fully explained to the employee exactly what he or she is supposed to do? Have I pointed out how work is to be done? Can I say for sure that there is no misunderstanding on these two points between the employee and me?
- Are my requirements for the employee the same as those for employees in similar jobs in my unit? Do these requirements compare favorably with those established by other supervisors for similar tasks? Are my requirements reasonable under the conditions? Am I consistent?
- Can I show clearly that I have seriously attempted to train the employee in the skills and knowledge needed to meet my requirements? Have I given enough time to develop the skills?
- Have I discussed the performance with the employee? Does the employee know that the performance is below that required for the job? Have I told the employee exactly what improvements must be made to meet the requirements?
- Have I followed administrative procedures? Have I notified the employee in writing of unsatisfactory performance and discussed what needs to be done to bring the work up to a satisfactory level?
- Am I prepared to defend my actions before my superiors, top management, and perhaps a hearing officer?

Points to Remember

- Job discipline is essential.
- Correcting an employee's behavior is more important than fixing blame for it.
- Problems affect employee performance both on and off the job.
- Sudden or abrupt changes in behavior can be indications of important employee problems.
- Problems should be dealt with as soon as possible after they have been identified.
- Disciplining an employee should be resorted to only after the supervisor is sure that training or counseling will not be helpful.
- Disciplinary actions must be documented.
- The action should be based on facts rather than on personal feelings.
- Disciplinary steps should be taken in order, and snap judgments or decisions based on impatience should be avoided.

HRIII-1.FRM

Performance Appraisal Form—Nonexempt

Name:	Job title:	Grade:	Date:
Location:		Department:	
• Annual • Midyear • New employee			

PERFORMANCE STANDARDS

KNOWLEDGE OF JOB: *A clear understanding of the facts or the factors required in the job.*

- Outstanding
- Above standard
- Meets standard
- Below standard

QUALITY OF WORK: *Accuracy and completeness of work*

- Outstanding
- Above standard
- Meets standard
- Below standard

PRODUCTIVITY: *Number of accomplishments, volume, and value*

- Outstanding
- Above standard
- Meets standard
- Below standard

DEPENDABILITY: *Conscientious, responsible, reliable; work completed on time*

- Outstanding
- Above standard
- Meets standard
- Below standard

COOPERATION: *Ability and willingness to work with associates, supervisors, and others*

- Outstanding
- Above standard
- Meets standard
- Below standard

OVERALL RATING   • Outstanding   • Above standard   • Meets standard   • Below standard

COMMENTS:

Position ready for now	Position ready for in 12 months

Mutual development plan:

Manager: _____   Employee: _____

Date: _____   Date: _____

HRIII-2.FRM

Performance Appraisal Form (A)—Exempt

Name:	Job title:	Grade:	Date:
Location:		Department:	
• Annual • Midyear • New employee			

PERFORMANCE EVALUATION

Knowledge: Comprehension of basic principles, techniques—has know-how.

Excellent comprehension in All areas	Comprehension in most areas	Satisfactory comprehension	Not well-informed
•	•	•	•

Describe:

Analytical ability and judgment: Obtains adequate facts; appraises and applies good judgment to the solution of problems.

Has keen insights— makes right decision	Good problem solver— has facts and uses judgment	Satisfactory decisions— sound judgment	Makes decisions without preparation or adequate information
•	•	•	•

Describe:

Planning and organization: Ability to plan own work to ensure efficient use of time; establishes goals and priorities. Gets things done on time.

Organized— makes use of time	Meets most deadlines— good use of time	Meets schedules and objectives satisfactorily	Poorly organized
•	•	•	•

Describe:

Quality of work: Performs assignments creatively, conscientiously, and accurately with high standards of quality and overall effectiveness.

Highest quality— error-free work	Quality work—can be relied on to be error-free	Satisfactory—turns out accurate work	Poor quality—work needs inspections
•	•	•	•

Describe:

Human relations skills: Gets along with others extremely well—uses tact and diplomacy. Maintains respect and confidence without trying to control.

Excellent—respected, not feared	Very good—seldom has criticisms or grievances	Satisfactory—maintains positive work environment	Lacks tact— controls rather than supports
•	•	•	•

Describe:

Performance Appraisal Form (A)—Exempt, p. 2

Supervisory ability: Organizes, coordinates, motivates, and develops through responsibility, authority, and recognition. Gets work done through others.			
Excellent–leader and manager, not controller •	Capable and competent •	Satisfactory—works well with people •	Lacks leadership— frequent problems •

Describe:

Budget and cost control: Uses all resources economically. Looks for ways to eliminate nonvalued activity and offers cost-reduction ideas.			
Excellent use of resources— reduces unneeded work •	Good use of assets •	Satisfactory—stays within budget •	Routinely exceeds budget— does not control costs •

	Met Expectations	
PERFORMANCE OBJECTIVES FROM PREVIOUS 12 MONTHS	Yes	No

PERFORMANCE OBJECTIVES FOR NEXT 12 MONTHS	Completion Date

OVERALL RATING
- Outstanding
- Above standard
- Meets standard
- Below standard

Position ready for now	Position ready for in 12 months

Mutual development plan:

Manager: _____ Employee: _____

Date: _____ Date: _____

HRIII-3.FRM   **Performance Appraisal Form (B)—Exempt**

Name:	Job title:	Grade:	Date:
Location:		Department:	
Annual Midyear New employee			

PERFORMANCE EVALUATION

LIST BELOW THE MAJOR OR MAIN DUTIES OF THE JOB IN ORDER OF PRIORITY. AFTER
EACH MAIN DUTY, APPRAISE THE PERFORMANCE OF THE EMPLOYEE—BE SPECIFIC.

Duty:
Appraisal:

Duty:
Appraisal:

Duty:
Appraisal

LIST BELOW THE MAJOR OR MAIN OBJECTIVES OF THE JOB IN ORDER OF PRIORITY. AFTER EACH MAIN
OBJECTIVE, APPRAISE THE PERFORMANCE OF THE EMPLOYEE—BE SPECIFIC.

Key objective:
Appraisal:

Key objective:
Appraisal:

Performance Appraisal Form (B)—Exempt, p. 2

HOW COULD IMPROVEMENT BE ACHIEVED IN ACCOMPLISHMENT OF DUTIES AND COMPLETION OF
OBJECTIVES?

WHAT FURTHER INFORMATION, TRAINING, OR EDUCATION ARE NEEDED TO FILL THE REQUIREMENTS OF THIS
JOB?

WHAT EXPECTATIONS FOR PROMOTION DOES THE EMPLOYEE HAVE AND HOW CAN THESE BE ATTAINED?

WHAT COMMENTS DO YOU HAVE REGARDING WORK PERFORMANCE OF THE EMPLOYEE OR QUALITY OF THE
WORK?

EMPLOYEE COMMENTS—DIFFERENCES OF OPINION OR PERFORMANCE MISUNDERSTANDINGS.

Sample Performance Appraisal Form (B)—Exempt, p. 3

DETAIL MUTUALLY AGREED-UPON PERFORMANCE IMPROVEMENT PLAN.

FURTHER COMMENTS AND REMARKS.

OVERALL RATING
☐ Outstanding   ☐ Above standard   ☐ Meets standard   ☐ Below standard

Position ready for now	Position ready for in 12 months

Manager: _____   Employee: _____

Date: _____   Date: _____

HRIII-4.FRM　　　　**Annual Performance Expectations**

Position:	Department:	
Name:	Title:	
Supervisor:		

Priority	Key responsibilities/accountabilities/objectives	How Measured	Completion Date
1.			
2.			
3.			
4.			
5.			
6.			
7.			

_____　　_____　　_____
Supervisor's Signature　　　Employee's Signature　　　　Date

CHAPTER IV

COMPENSATION AND BENEFITS

For the purposes of this discussion, the term "compensation" refers to direct pay and benefits or total compensation. Compensation is the most substantial cost faced by most employers. The role of benefits in a company is often misunderstood by employees, and employees do not take full advantage of those the company provides. This is a major mistake, because the cost of providing benefits in many cases is close to 50 percent of the payroll.

Over the last 20 years, workplace changes have challenged the traditional approach to determining pay and benefits. Managers may question whether the pay and benefits system helps the company achieve its objectives. When employees see the large bonuses for executives and compare their pay, they question whether the company values their contributions.

Traditionally, when companies needed to develop a formal compensation structure, they copied one used by another company or hired a consultant to develop one specifically for their company. When they needed to revise their pay schedules, they surveyed similar companies in the area and established pay rates and salaries based on those in the market. Inflation and the rising cost of living were devaluing real earnings, so companies initiated an automatic increase based on the Consumer Price Index. This increase became institutionalized as a cost-of-living adjustment (COLA).

Then someone suggested that companies should link an individual's pay to individual or department objectives, and pay for performance became a rallying cry for both employees and managers. The "carrot-and-stick" theory became a standard for compensation management. However, the scheme does not guarantee company profitability and often focuses on short-term accomplishments instead of long-term viability, and problems can arise when companies award bigger increases to productive employees than to an employee who appears less competent.

Then global competitiveness entered the picture. Many U.S. businesses had inflated ranks of management and administrative personnel, which made them unprofitable. Since salary increases did not increase company profitability, businesses found they could no longer afford annual increases of 10 to 15 percent. Thus, salary increases were no longer sufficient to motivate employees; instead, they contributed to employee dissatisfaction.

Now many companies try to compensate employees using some form of base pay with additional direct incentives. The successful incentive plans reward employees based on mutually accepted standards. Some are short-lived because they reward the wrong behaviors, and internal inequities may keep employees from accomplishing the desired results. One of the biggest problems is that companies reward top management for achieving short-term financial goals rather than long-term viability. Downsizing the workforce and closing facilities can help a business achieve profitability targets, but studies show that these companies seldom rebound to their former greatness as thriving businesses. Huge executive bonuses have generated considerable criticism because they are often not linked to company performance.

Employees often perceive benefits as something other than compensation, and employers miss the opportunity to market benefits as part of the total compensation package. Thirty years ago, most companies focused exclusively on securing long-term employees. Today, companies still try to provide competitive benefits to attract employees, but they have a critical need to control costs. These conflicting objectives regularly cause dilemmas. With economic conditions as they are, employees see their benefit package as the one aspect of the job that they can count on. Employers facing inflation do not necessarily want to cut benefits, but they have a critical need to limit cost increases.

Many employees see benefits as entitlements. Because of the rush to provide the maximum affordable benefits, employees no longer see them as a reward for participating in activities that improve company profitability. In fact, studies have shown that as employees secure more benefits, they see less of a relationship among the benefits they receive, their responsibility to the company, and the value of their contributions. As a result, employees see themselves as entitled to benefits rather than having earned them. Employers must find ways to return to using benefits as compensation for employee contributions.

Forms of Compensation

Figure IV-1 outlines the compensation matrix. Compensation may be direct, as cash (wages, bonuses, incentives, administrative increases), or indirect, through services and benefits (pensions, health insurance, vacations, workers' compensation, Social Security, etc.).

Figure IV-1. Compensation and Benefits

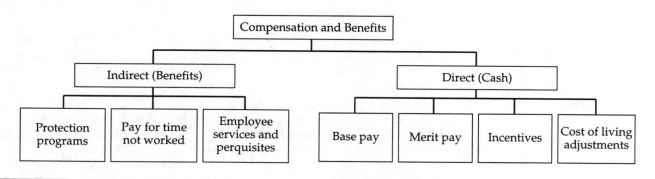

In starting a human resource function, the compensation and benefits process must be addressed. Top management usually identifies this process as a major concern. They may be concerned with external competitiveness, want to increase their own pay, or have concerns about employees' perception of the fairness of the pay scale. Employees might be signaling their dissatisfaction through high turnover, formal complaints, responses to employee surveys, or the grapevine. The company might be unable to recruit skilled employees. Compensation and benefits are not areas to modify without much study, planning, communication, and careful analysis of the expectations of both management and employees. Sometimes, doing nothing is the best choice!

It is crucially important that all aspects of a company's reward and recognition strategy be coordinated, or—as many companies have found—the return on the investment will not exceed the overall compensation expense and the cost of administration.

Direct Compensation

The compensation objectives outlined in **Figure IV-2** are applicable in practically every company. How do companies develop pay processes that meet these objectives?

There are three parts to a pay model for a company: (1) the policies that form the foundation of the system; (2) the techniques that make up the specific operations; and (3) the objectives.

Figure IV-2. Direct Compensation Objectives

- Identify prevailing market wages and salaries.
- Pay competitive wages and salaries considering company profitability.
- Increase employee satisfaction with company reward strategy.
- Maintain a strict relationship between value of the work performed and employees' value to the organization.
- Identify best methods and techniques for awarding pay increases while restraining the ability of managers to grant unwarranted increases.
- Reward levels and types of performance that add to the profitability of the company.

Pay Policies

Most companies adopt one of three pay policies (see **Figure IV-3**). They serve as the foundation on which pay systems are designed and administered.

Figure IV-3. Pay Policies and Techniques

Policies	Techniques		Objectives
External competitiveness	Market surveys	Pay levels	
Internal equity	Job analysis	Pay structure	Efficiency Equity
Employee characteristics and contributions	Seniority Performance Increase guidelines Incentives		

External competitiveness

External competitiveness or equity refers to how an employer pays compared with what similar companies are paying. Policy determination on pay often requires some hard decisions. How much do other employers pay line supervisors or HR managers? How much does the company want to pay line supervisors or HR managers? Some companies may want to set their pay levels higher than those of their competitors, hoping to remain union-free or to attract better employees. Some may offer lower base pay but a greater opportunity to get overtime, better benefits, or a better incentive plan.

Pay and benefits might be lower in a company that instead offers job security or excellent supervision.

Internal equity

Internal equity refers to comparisons among jobs or skill levels inside the company. Pay relationships that are internally consistent are based on the content of the work, the skills required, and the relative contribution of the work to the company's overall objectives. How does the work of an executive secretary compare with the work of an accounting clerk, a computer operator, or a word processing supervisor? Which jobs require more skill, experience, human relations expertise, or ability to communicate effectively? Does the output from one job add more value to the company's bottom line than that from another? Internal consistency is hard to achieve in determining pay both for those doing similar work and for those performing different tasks. It causes more dissatisfaction than any other approach to compensation, including external equity.

Employee characteristics and contributions

Under this pay policy, the emphasis is placed on individual performance or seniority. Should all employees doing the same work receive the same base pay? Should one employee be paid more than another based on seniority or superior individual performance? Should managers and supervisors be paid based on the performance of the department they supervise or the company overall? Should they be paid based on achieving short-term goals?

Compensation Techniques

Figure IV-3 shows compensation techniques used to link pay policies to compensation objectives.

External competitiveness

Market surveys. These reveal what other employers are paying for similar experience and skills. Generally, companies try to find organizations in their own area with which to compare themselves. If there are few or no competitors or companies with similar jobs in close proximity, they may go outside the local area for survey data. The three attributes to look for when selecting companies for a market survey are similar jobs, similar size, and similar geographic location.

Companies use several techniques for conducting salary surveys. Personal interviews usually garner the most accurate responses, but they are also usually the most expensive. Mailed surveys are probably the most frequently used and the cheapest; however, the jobs must be clearly defined or the results may not be accurate. Companies receiving a mail salary survey may delegate its completion to a lower level clerical person. Allowing for discretion in the survey instrument invites inaccuracies. Many companies validate mail responses with telephone follow-up inquiries.

Companies usually do not seek market data for all jobs but only for benchmark positions that can be easily compared across company lines. These key jobs typically are chosen because (1) work content is stable over time, (2) many employees are in these positions, (3) concentrations of minorities and females are unlikely, and (4) similar positions are commonly found in the employment community. Once the market data have been received and summarized, the results can help translate the notion of external competitiveness into actual pay practices.

Pay levels. These decisions start with determining the relationship between policy lines and company pay objectives. The company should decide if it wants to pay above the market (lead), with the market (match), or below the market. If the company wants to attract experienced employees with high potential, it may have to pay above the market. If the compensation objective is to reduce turnover, retain valued employees, or reduce dissatisfaction with pay, it should either match or lead the market.

Many compensation professionals believe that leading the market in pay allows the company to attract and retain the cream of the applicants and that these higher quality employees will be more productive. However, research does not support these beliefs. Anecdotal evidence from HR and quality consultants suggests that higher pay does not necessarily result in increased productivity. An example is a large Midwest telecommunications company that leads the market significantly in pay for most job categories. Among professionals and management, turnover is almost 20 percent annually; among nonexempt and hourly categories, it has been approximately 35 percent. (A 12 percent rate of turnover is normal.)

If the sole compensation objective is to contain labor costs, paying below the market has traditionally been the technique used. However, paying below the market may cause serious employee relations and compensation problems that typically cost much more than was saved in wages.

Internal equity

Job analysis and job description. This systematic process collects information about jobs. Companies use a position description questionnaire to decide the essential functions of the job, the frequency of activity, and the priority for each function. Job analysis data are summarized into a standard format called the *job description*. This description typically contains three sections that identify, define, and describe the job.

1. Identify the job by its title, the number of people holding the job, whether it is exempt or nonexempt from the overtime provisions of the Fair Labor Standards Act, and to whom the incumbents report.

2. Define the job by identifying the purpose of the job, the criteria for satisfactory performance, and how this job fits in with other jobs and company objectives.

3. Describe the job content by discussing the major duties of the incumbent, the specific work to be done, the supervision required, and the discretion allowed. Content should also include the training and experience required for the job.

Since the implementation of the Americans with Disabilities Act (ADA) only essential job requirements may be used to decide qualifications for positions. Requirements for physical activity should be included only if they are essential job functions. As a practical matter, most jobs have some physical requirements, but few have physical requirements that cannot be reasonably adapted.

Systematic *evaluation* of the job description helps maintain pay structures by comparing the similarities and differences in the content and value of jobs. When properly designed and administered, job evaluation can also help ensure that pay structures are internally equitable and acceptable to the employer and employee. Job evaluation can have four functions, depending on how the process is designed and administered:

1. To classify or group jobs based on similarities and differences in their work content.
2. To establish a job hierarchy based on the relative value of jobs.
3. As an administrative procedure linking internal job content with external market rates.
4. As a tool for measurement and negotiation over pay rates.

The four fundamental job evaluation methods are ranking, classification, factor comparison, and the point method (see **Figure IV-4**).

Because of political pressure, especially in smaller companies, conducting valid job evaluations without independent outside assistance is extremely difficult. Frequently, even large companies cannot overcome managers' desire to overrate and inflate the value of certain jobs to reward steady or favorite employees.

Pay structure. This focuses attention on the link between employee perceptions and their work behaviors. Pay differences induce employees to join a company, undertake training, progress through jobs, meet performance expectations, and continue (or not continue) employment with the company. Traditionally, pay structures were based on steep hierarchial progressions, with unskilled laborers receiving the lowest pay. Top managers with broad responsibilities and many employees to manage were paid the most. In between were technical employees, salespeople, and professionals. Supervisors were paid more than their peers who performed the activity. This hierarchy led to an explosion of unneeded management and supervisory personnel, because in these systems the only way to improve pay was to become a manager.

Figure IV-4. Job Evaluation Methods

Method	Description	Disadvantage
Ranking	Ranks jobs according to their relative value. The simplest, fastest, easiest to understand, and least expensive.	Simple definitions result in subjective opinions, difficult to explain or justify. Requires users to be knowledgeable about every job.
Classification	Involves slotting jobs into a series of classes and grades covering all jobs in the company. Widely used in the public sector and in engineering, technical, and scientific jobs in the private sector.	Each class must be described generally enough to slot several jobs, yet specifically enough to have meaning.
Factor comparison	Involves evaluating jobs on the basis of two criteria: (1) a set of compensable factors, and (2) market wages or points for a selected set of jobs.	Very complex. Limited usefulness.
Point method	Assigns points for three features: (1) compensable factors, (2) a scale of factors, and (3) weights reflecting the importance of each factor. Total points for all jobs are calculated and a hierarchy is established. Once implemented, it is easy to administer.	Very complex. Must be communicated clearly to managers and supervisors.

Little has been written about employees' perception of equitable pay among jobs. Some companies, notably Ben and Jerry's Ice Cream, have reduced the spread between top management and the lowest paid employees. Japanese companies such as Sony minimize the direct differences between top and bottom while providing significant perks to executives. Some innovative and creative companies such as Nucor Steel minimize the importance of base pay and build teamwork by basing most compensation on company profitability.

Why not just pay market rates? Although certain key jobs might be comparable across several companies, not all jobs are alike. Setting pay rates for dissimilar jobs using market data is difficult. The solution is to set pay rates for key jobs and slot other jobs around them. This slotting is accomplished by evaluating jobs.

Employee characteristics

Several additional factors go into determining pay for individual employees. The two basic factors are (1) Should different employees holding the same job be paid the same? and (2) What factors should be used to recognize differences between employees?

Seniority. When employers do not wish to differentiate between individual performance, or where there is a collective bargaining unit, often one flat rate is paid for a particular job or class of jobs. The existence of a flat rate does not mean that performance or experience differences among employees do not exist, but that the employer chooses not to consider these variations. However, even in these companies, seniority or tenure is often used as a pay differential.

Performance. Most employees have come to expect annual pay increases, even when the business has not been profitable. Top executives even expect to receive increases and bonuses for not losing as much money as they did in the previous year! The tradition of basing pay increases on performance is well established; however, annual pay increases are often disguised by calling them performance-based or merit increases. The idea is that lower performance ratings are tied to lower pay increases, while higher ratings result in larger increases. The problem is that managers may use performance ratings as a device to justify awarding a pay increase.

Some studies have shown few mutually agreeable and satisfying processes for linking individual performance to pay increases. For example, many managers object to trying to give employees a performance rating when the employees do not control the resources that determine the success of their performance.

Annual guidelines. The *general increase* is typically found in unionized companies. A contract is negotiated that specifies some equal percentage increase across all job classifications for each year of the agreement. A *cost-of-living adjustment* is triggered by an increase in the Consumer Price Index; the same percentage increase applies to all covered positions. *Performance-based* and *merit increases* are discussed above. *Lump sum payments* are often used by companies to reward employees who have reached the top of their salary range. The benefit to the company is that high-performing employees can be rewarded without inflating the salary range.

Incentives. *Incentives* are different from annual increases because they are usually distributed irregularly and do not form a basis for future increases. The two varieties are group incentives and individual incentives.

Piecework rates guarantee employees an hourly rate for doing the minimum. The employee is paid more according to how much faster he or she works. Many companies still use piecework rates as an alternative to a formal appraisal process or as a motivational device. Retail sales associates are often paid a guaranteed hourly rate, with a certain dollar volume of sales required to keep the position. Even professional firms (accounting, engineering, and law) often have a minimum volume of sales required for continued employment. The employee receives a salary based on that minimum; if individual sales do not reach the minimum, the employee might be terminated.

Commissions are commonly found in sales jobs. Straight commission is typically a percentage of the price of the item. A variation is for a company to pay a small salary and also a commission or bonus when a minimum sales goal is achieved. With commission sales, there is usually a small draw against earnings or very limited base pay. Commission sales are more prevalent in some industries than others.

Administration

It is possible to design a system that integrates external equity, internal equity, and employee characteristics, but the system cannot meet its objectives unless it is administered properly. Administration includes planning the elements that should be included (short-term versus long-term incentives), talking with employees, evaluating the system, assessing the competency and validity of supervisors' actions involving pay, and changing the system when it needs improvement.

Do employees see the system as fair? Do they understand which factors will be considered in setting pay? Do they have channels for raising questions and voicing complaints about pay? How do better performing companies pay their employees? Such information is necessary to evaluate and redesign a system, to adjust to changes, and to highlight potential problem areas.

Planning

Properly designed and administered compensation processes help managers achieve their objectives. Many managers do not see controlling costs and forecasting compensation requirements as important. They say, "If we have the money, let's give it to them." This approach will not make a company profitable. A properly planned compensation process will reduce the ability of managers to award inconsistent and unearned increases. It will improve employees' perception that individuals are rewarded for their performance. It will allow the employer to control compensation costs. It supports a culture in which employees perceive the company as a good place to work. In the planning process, the top salary should be paid for activities that produce the most value for the company. It is work output that is valued and paid for.

Budgeting

Instructing managers in the use of the compensation system—its objectives, policies, and techniques—is crucial. Most managers believe their employees deserve more than is available for pay increases. During the budgeting process, managers may try to play games with the numbers, undermining the process. They need to understand that properly developed budgets offer many benefits and contributions to the company's profitability. Budgeting enables managers to foresee the financial impact of pay increases on profitability.

Communication

Some managers take a positive approach to talking about the compensation process. They know that a pay process can influence behaviors and attitudes. Pay differentials can influence employees to seek better positions, obtain additional training, and gain experience. If employees do not perceive the system as based on work-related and logical processes, they will be dissatisfied. Communicating the process eliminates this problem.

Evaluation

Employee dissatisfaction with pay is costly. It erodes commitment to work and often leads to absenteeism, high turnover, low productivity, increased number of grievances, and other management problems. However, more pay is seldom the solution to these problems. Regularly evaluating the effectiveness of the process is important.

Laws relating to compensation

The Fair Labor Standards Act (FLSA) is a federal law that sets the minimum wage and requirements for paying overtime. The minimum wage is currently $4.25 per hour. All employees covered by FLSA (nonexempt employees) must be paid time-and-a-half their regular rate for any hours worked over 40 in a work week. Executive, professional, and administrative employees who are not covered by FLSA (exempt employees) do not have to be paid overtime. There is a substantial body of law and administrative ruling covering the payment of overtime, exempt status, and minimum wage. See appendixes A and B for more information on this subject.

Indirect Compensation

So far, the discussion has focused on direct pay or cash compensation. The balance of this chapter will discuss the design and implementation of indirect pay processes or benefits. These include health protection, insurance, retirement income, paid time away from work, and employee services.

Objectives and Strategies

Typically, benefits are expected to accomplish four objectives: (1) to foster external competitiveness, (2) to increase cost-effectiveness, (3) to meet employees' needs and preferences, and (4) to comply with federal laws. Executives and human resource professionals have expressed concern about the belief that the more benefits offered, the more productive the employee. Although the lack of commonly provided benefits can result in employee dissatisfaction, more benefits do not necessarily result in productive and profitable employees. Employee studies have consistently shown that it isn't the number of benefits but the ability to choose what best fits the employee's situation that determines satisfaction with benefits. A survey by a major benefits consulting company found that more than 70 percent of the respondents would stay with a company that had good benefits, even if they hated their jobs and the company. How well spent are the financial resources used to "buy" employee retention? **Figure IV-5** illustrates the decisions managers face in developing a benefits program.

Figure IV-5. Basic Benefit Decisions

Competitiveness: How should benefits compare with those of competitors?

Coverage: Which benefits should be offered? Which benefits are mandatory?

Communication: How can the company inform employees about their benefits?

Choice: What degree of choice or flexibility should be included?

Competitiveness

Just as with direct compensation, companies need to position their total compensation package, including benefits, in the marketplace. Most large companies compare their benefits with those of similar companies. Beware of management in small and emerging companies who try to offer benefits they want for themselves rather than focusing on matching the market and the competition. Assessing competitors' benefits programs is valuable, but a company's own program should not exceed its ability to pay. The four comparisons to make are (1) total cost of benefits, (2) cost per employee, (3) percentage of payroll, and (4) cost per employee per hour.

Optional Benefits

Four kinds of benefits are typically provided to employees: paid time away from work, life and health insurance, employee services, and retirement income. Some benefits are legally mandated, such as unemployment insurance, workers' compensation, and Social Security. Companies often do not track the cost of these benefits, mistakenly believing they would be paying the salary anyway or that the cost is small compared with other labor costs. However, in many large companies, the cost of benefits exceeds 40 percent of payroll and is fast approaching 50 percent. Many companies offer a "cafeteria plan" of benefits and offer employees choices among the benefits offered.

Paid time away from work

Employers usually offer pay for holidays and vacations; sometimes they pay for sick leave. Neither managers nor employees see the real cost of providing these benefits. If the position is really needed, any time away from work means something is not getting completed or someone else has been assigned to do the work and the company is paying double.

Insurance

Three major forms of insurance are common: health, disability-accident, and life. *Health insurance* is extremely costly and very popular with employees. Coverage may include prescription drugs, mental health services, and dental care. In spite of cost-containment efforts by both employers and the government, health care costs continue to escalate dramatically. *Group life insurance* is generally very inexpensive; however, for most employees, life insurance is a low priority. *Long-term and short-term sickness and accident or disability insurance* protects employees who have accidents or injuries off the job that leave them temporarily or permanently unable to work.

Employee services

"Employee services" is a catchall category for a variety of voluntary benefits, such as cafeterias, saunas and gyms, health club memberships, commuter vans, discounts on company products, and child care.

Educational programs. Many organizations provide education assistance for employees. The coverage varies considerably for everything from job-related training to degree and advanced degree programs. Educational support is often part of the employee development program. Congress has been toying with eliminating the tax-exempt status of education programs, but most companies would continue them regardless of tax status.

Social and recreational programs. Many companies are finding that wellness and recreational programs increase productivity and reduce health care costs. Some—such as smoking cessation and employee assistance programs—have significant, proven cost-cutting benefits; others—such as in-house gyms—may not have the same return on the investment.

Child care. Some employers support on-premise child care centers, but there are serious disadvantages. Most companies that offer a child care benefit subsidize the cost but do not actually operate the center. Many offer referral programs, assisting employees in finding suitable child care arrangements.

Retirement income

Employees' retirement income comes from four sources—Social Security benefits, private pensions, investment income, and earnings.

Retirement (pension) plans. The Employee Retirement Income Security Act (ERISA) (1974) and subsequent federal tax legislation have subjected qualified pension and other benefit plans to comprehensive government control. The purpose of this law and subsequent amendments is to ensure that employees who put money into retirement plans and depend on them for retirement funds actually will receive the money when they retire.

Qualified plans. Qualified plans must (1) be in writing and communicated to employees; (2) be established for the exclusive benefit of employees or their beneficiaries; (3) satisfy rules concerning eligibility, vesting, and funding; and (4) not discriminate in terms of contributions or benefits in favor of officers, shareholders, or highly compensated employees. Qualified plans offer tax-favored benefits to both employers and employees. The plans may be either contributory or noncontributory.

- **Defined benefit plans.** The employer agrees to provide the employee with a retirement benefit amount based on a formula. The employer funds the plan and bears the responsibility for ensuring that sufficient funds will be available in the plan when they are required. The employee receives a predetermined amount upon retirement.

- **Defined contribution plan.** The employer pays a specific amount into the pension fund for each participant. This contribution may be a percentage of salary or a percentage of profits. Once the employer has made the contribution, there is no further financial requirement. The amount of the benefit received by the employee upon retirement is determined by how the investment funds perform and is not guaranteed.

- **Deferred compensation.** Many companies offer deferred compensation programs such as 401(k) plans. These plans permit employees to postpone income taxes on part of their pay, if that portion is contributed by the employer to a qualified plan. Larger companies typically match part of the employees' contributions. Smaller companies and many professional firms do not match employees' contribution. Ongoing tax law revisions affect the attractiveness of these plans.

- **Employee stock ownership plan (ESOP).** In stock ownership plans, employers contribute to a trust that purchases company stock for employees. Employers get a tax deduction for the contributions and employees get equity in the company. Some studies have shown that employees may stay longer at companies that have an ESOP, at least until the company contributions are vested, but there is little evidence that employees are more productive or efficient. For many small and closely held companies, ESOPs are simply a tax-avoidance strategy.

- **Profit-sharing programs.** Profit sharing is the payment of a regular share of the company profits as a supplement to normal compensation. Such programs may be perceived as a group incentive process rather than an employee retirement strategy. The plans usually require the employee's share to be added to a company-controlled investment pool. Some plans are more flexible; however, since most plans use the maximum vesting period, employees commonly view profit sharing as a retirement strategy.

  The assumption (as with ESOPs) is that employees who have a direct interest in the profitability of the company will reduce waste and increase productivity. Some of these programs are successful, but many do not meet expectations. Studies have shown that if there is a frequent cash payout, plans do have some measure of success. If there is no cash payment, but the profits must be invested, the program seldom meets employee expectations.

  In closely held and small companies, profit sharing is touted by financial planners and public accountants as a tax-avoidance strategy. When this is the true objective, employees often sense the insincerity and recognize the program for what it is. Companies that are considering profit sharing should carefully assess their objectives and plan accordingly.

  Nonqualified plans. Federal law has made it difficult to use company benefits to compensate highly paid executives. One way for companies to provide additional benefits to key executives is to offer nonqualified deferred compensation plans. These plans are a promise by the employer to pay a given amount at a later date. Nonqualified plans are not deductible to the employer, nor are the benefits guaranteed to the individual.

Mandated Benefits

Employers are legally required to offer certain benefits to employees; these include Social Security, unemployment compensation, and workers' compensation. The employee and the employer have little or no discretion over these benefits.

Social Security

The Social Security Act of 1935 created a system designed to prevent the severe financial hardship that many elderly people suffer on retirement. Covered employees are compelled to pay a certain percentage of their annual income to the system throughout their working careers, and employers must match this amount. At retirement age, the contributors become eligible to receive payments from the general Social Security fund. When people refer to "Social Security," they normally are referring to Old-Age, Survivors, and Disability Insurance (OASDI). OASDI is the compulsory retirement program; all but a very few working Americans contribute to and are covered by OASDI. Taxes paid into the Social Security fund are governed by the provisions of the Federal Insurance Contribution Act.

Eligibility for benefits is based on the number of quarters of coverage an individual has been credited with during employment. There are three categories:

1. *Fully insured status* grants eligibility for all types of old-age and survivor benefits. For an individual to achieve fully insured status, quarters of coverage must equal or exceed the number of years since 1950 or since age 21.

2. *Insured status* grants eligibility for some survivor benefits. It requires at least 6 quarters of coverage in the 13-quarter period ending with death, disability, or the attainment of age 62.

3. *Disability status* grants eligibility for benefits. It requires at least 20 quarters of coverage in the 40 quarters preceding disablement.

Benefit amounts are calculated by means of a complicated formula that is modified annually to account for cost-of-living increases. The benefit formulas are heavily weighted in favor of lower income contributors.

HR professionals should have a general understanding of Social Security to answer employee questions, understand to whom and under what circumstances benefits are payable, and encourage employees to plan for their retirement.

Unemployment compensation insurance

Unemployment insurance is established by state statutes prompted by a federal tax. All covered employers pay federal unemployment tax. Employers who contribute to a federally approved state system are relieved of paying to the federal government an amount equal to their state contributions, up to 90 percent of the state tax. Thus, if a state did not enact an approved plan, employers in the state would pay the same tax, but employed workers would get no benefits. For this reason, all states have unemployment insurance systems.

The premium paid by employers is based on each company's experience rating (claims filed by its employees). An employer with a good record can substantially reduce its tax, while a company with a high turnover rate will pay more. This system encourages employers to keep turnover low and to oppose unemployment compensation claims. Eligible employees must have worked a specified amount of time and must be available and actively seeking work. Employees may be disqualified if they refuse to accept suitable employment.

HR professionals often take the unemployment compensation process lightly and do not contest benefit claims. If the employer can prove that the employee quit or was dismissed because of job-related misconduct, unemployment benefits can be reduced or denied. Such action not only reduces the company's experience rating but also sends a message to employees who might be considering quitting and filing for unemployment compensation.

Workers' compensation insurance

Workers' compensation insurance statutes establish a process through which employees who are injured on the company's premises or while performing duties within the scope of employment are covered for medical costs and for their disability. Employees are entitled to benefits regardless of fault or the employer's liability. The benefit for employers is that liability is limited by the schedule set by state regulations.

Workers' compensation insurance is a state system, and benefits vary considerably from state to state. Payments for hospital and medical expenses and rehabilitation services are normally included. Injured employees may also receive compensation for lost wages and for permanent partial disability. The system is generally funded through private insurance, self-insurance, or payment into a state fund. The amount paid by each employer is determined by various factors, including type of industry, type of work performed, and previous accident rate. All states require that every company with employees be covered. If an employee is injured and the company does not have workers' compensation insurance, the company may be subject to general personal injury liability without limits and may be assessed severe penalties by the state.

Additional information can be found in chapter VII, in the SHRM *Publications Catalog*, and through SHRM's Information Center.

Flexible Benefits

Traditionally, employees were involved in their benefits program only to the extent of being asked to choose among options offered by the employer. Today employees are involved in choosing not only the types of benefits offered but also the components for which they will pay. Surveys have shown that with increased participation and involvement, benefits programs are more responsive to employees' needs and employees are more satisfied with them.

Generally, companies mandate a certain level of health and life insurance and some minimal level of retirement contribution. The company generally pays the full cost of these benefits. The company then offers a cash contribution from which the employee may choose additional health, life, or retirement benefits. Some companies require that the contribution be used within specific guidelines; others allow employees to use this amount for benefits without any restriction. Employees may choose more life insurance, dependent health care, long-term disability insurance, or dental coverage. Some companies allow employees to use the cash for child care services, add it to their retirement investments, or even buy additional vacation time or days off.

The advantage of flexible benefits is that employees can choose those that fit their needs. Someone with a family might choose additional coverage, while a single person might want to put money into more days off. The disadvantage is that the tax treatment of flexible benefits plans is subject to the whims of Congress and to changing Internal Revenue Service regulations. A flexible benefits plan requires a significant amount of administrative time, which may be outsourced to a plan administrator. Also, because of the wide choice of benefits, the cost of individual components of the plan may increase dramatically in one area. For example, if employees with many medical expenses are the only ones to choose an enhanced health plan, the cost of that plan is likely to rise.

Many companies, even very large ones, are beginning to rethink their benefits contribution process. Rather than increasing their contribution, more companies are allocating a small cash contribution and supplementing it with additional cash bonuses based on profitability. This eliminates the need to meet all the benefits cost increases.

Whatever option the company chooses, it must inform employees and ensure that they understand the total compensation process. Several years ago, a large telecommunications company unilaterally implemented a flexible benefits plan. The major union (Communication Workers of America), which had previously been unsuccessful in efforts to organize the company, suddenly found enough support to launch a major organizational campaign. In another municipal organization, the city's unilateral decision to change health insurance carriers within the flexible benefits program caused several employees to seek union representation.

CHAPTER V

POLICIES AND PROCEDURES, EMPLOYEE HANDBOOKS, AND PERSONNEL FILES

Policies and Procedures

The law requires human resource policies. For example, the federal Equal Employment Opportunity Act, authorized by the Civil Rights Act of 1964, requires two specific policies: a policy on discrimination against certain protected class members and a policy on sexual harassment in the workplace. Other federal laws requiring policies are the Family and Medical Leave Act of 1993 (FMLA), the Employee Retirement Income Security Act of 1974, and the Fair Labor Standards Act of 1938, which establishes minimum wage requirements. States also have requirements concerning workers' compensation insurance coverage, safety regulations (such as minimum age for operating hazardous equipment), and occasionally state minimum wage. Cities often have additional requirements, such as equal access to public accommodations, and sometimes even separate nondiscrimination requirements. A company needs to know all state and local requirements that affect it; however, if one starts by identifying general human resource requirements and adds federal law requirements, most issues will be covered.

Definitions

A *policy* is a broad guideline to be followed under a given set of circumstances. Policies are written so that managers can easily grasp their intent and take the necessary action. Good policies are based on good judgment, good management practices, and common sense. They are perceived as fair and consistent. Policies often appear in employee handbooks to give general direction on management's expectations of employees.

A *procedure* is a sequence of steps for accomplishing an objective. Procedures may further interpret or define how a policy should be carried out; they might be considered the rules for certain actions or nonactions. While policies are written for general distribution as a guide to employees, procedures are generally written for the use of managers and supervisors.

Some companies create comprehensive policies that cover every conceivable aspect of management activity, while others focus on basic areas and leave broad discretion to managers. Some consultants and employee relations lawyers have advised against having policies and procedures, but most HR professionals recommend written policies, although "less is better."

The Need for Policies

Policies govern the execution of various activities in an organization and provide guidance for making decisions and taking action on a variety of employee-related activities. Carefully developed policies are vital to the successful management of human resources. If one management action destroys employee productivity and morale, it is inconsistency in making decisions. Perceived unfair and unequal treatment is a major cause of employee relations lawsuits and discrimination charges.

Well-defined and appropriate policies serve to assure employees the company will treat them fairly and objectively and let employees know what is expected of them. Managers can resolve problems with a greater degree of confidence when there is an objective basis for their decisions. Policy statements can provide answers for employees to questions that might otherwise have to be referred to supervisors. Policy statements may also include the rationale for the policy.

Human resource policies must be closely integrated with policies relating to the operation of the business. For example, the policy of providing a union-free stabilized employee environment cannot be accomplished without coordinating sales, production, and transportation policies. A policy of encouraging a pro-employee, pro-family workplace cannot be accomplished without considering scheduling, flexible hours, the philosophy of management, and even the recruitment policy. A marketing objective of expanding sales into foreign countries or a focus on expanding sales into a minority population requires integration with human resource policies.

Fair and Consistent Treatment

Fair and consistent treatment of employees does not mean identical treatment. A degree of flexibility is necessary to allow for the circumstances surrounding any decision. An employee who has established a good work record and a cooperative attitude would not be treated as severely for violating a work rule as another employee with a poor record. Policies provide the limits within which some discretion is permitted.

The safest and least risky policy is also usually the strictest. For example, to reduce exposure to sexual harassment charges, the most reliable policy would be to restrict fraternization in the workplace. Although some states restrict the ability of companies to control the personal relationships of their employees, a strict policy will significantly reduce hostile work environment and sexual harassment difficulties. However, companies that want to be family-friendly may not want to prohibit employees (other than supervisors) from engaging in personal relationships. Some companies prohibit employees from supervising relatives. Other companies do not impose any such regulations.

Companies may legitimately decide on the severity of their policies. The key here is managers who clearly understand the flexibility and the limitations and who communicate deviations from policy across functional lines.

What Policies and Procedures Are Needed

A sample table of contents from an employee handbook can be used as a checklist of common policies and procedures (see **HRV-1.FRM**). Federal law requires some of these policies and procedures; some are discretionary. If the HR professional is not experienced working with policies and procedures, he or she should conduct further research or obtain professional assistance.

Human resources must orchestrate and coordinate, not mandate, the development of policies. Starting the policy development process without manager and employee input is a mistake, and the question of how far the company should go into specific areas should be decided by all managers, not only human resource professionals. Human resources sometimes functions as an advocate for employees and as the administrator of employee-related activities. In this capacity, human resources may have to encourage management to develop pro-employee policies and procedures that may restrict managers' discretion to treat employees as they wish. Conversely, human resources may need to oppose policies favored by management when the result would be a discouraged or demoralized workforce. Policies that are incorrectly designed and developed can easily have a damaging impact on an otherwise productive and committed workforce.

Developing Policies

How policies are developed is as important as which policies are set up. The following should be considered:

- A policy committee of representatives from all functional areas should be appointed. The committee does not have to consist entirely of managers; it may include representatives of different levels of employees, including nonexempt and hourly employees. (This committee might fall under the National Labor Relations Board rulings on employee participation committees. For further discussion, see the section on the safety committee in chapter VI.)

- The committee should have a clear charter that identifies the authority, responsibility, and process by which recommendations will be approved.

- If a cross-functional, multilevel committee is used, the committee charter might consider setting three policy approval levels. The first level would be for policies over which the committee has full responsibility and authority. Top management involvement would be limited to review for overall coordination and final approval. These policies might include starting and ending times, staffing and recruiting, improvement processes, training and education, and performance appraisal.

The second level might include policies that the committee has the power to recommend but on which the final decision rests with top management. Most policies fall into this group. Some policies—such as those for EEO and sexual harassment—allow for little modification, but they might be made more pertinent if the policy committee develops the exact wording. Policies on alternate dispute resolution, grievance resolution, safety, and Occupational Safety and Health Administration compliance might also fall into this group.

The third level would be those policies over which top management retains full discretion and authority. These include policies concerning pay and salary and what benefits to offer and how to administer them.

- The main objective of the policy committee is to review all current policies for validity, consistency, and legal compliance; suggest additional policies essential for company operation; and decide which should be deleted or revised. Only policies that are required and absolutely necessary should be considered for inclusion.

- A policy statement should explain the reason for the policy, the date it becomes effective, and when it should be reviewed. Some policy requirements remain consistent; for example, nondiscrimination and sexual harassment policies, once developed and implemented, will remain very much the same. Other policies, such as those on compensation and benefits, should be reviewed regularly or, at the very least, annually.

Policies developed and implemented in this manner are clear to employees, usually have the full support of all employees (including managers), and are likely to be followed, resulting in fewer problems and complaints.

Many management consultants and employment lawyers write policies and procedures for companies. Having professional assistance in this task is important. However, in developing and writing policies, two points are important: (1) policies must be focused on strategy and related to company operation, and (2) they must be discussed with and understood by the employees and managers.

A company should not choose policies from a checklist. It should assess its actual needs and then decide what policies are necessary. They should be written in plain language, not in legalese. Certain phases or words have legal meanings—they have been found by the courts to mean certain certain things. One of these phrases is "with just cause," which used to be common in policies on discharge and termination. The courts have interpreted this phrase as requiring a legally acceptable reason for the termination, which often is more than employers thought should be required. A company may want to have certain policies reviewed by legal counsel or written in legal terms. However, the human resource professional should use caution when using consultants, lawyers, or personnel policy software to develop policies. Policies written in legalese are of no value if the employees and managers do not understand their intent, purposes, or guidelines.

Employee Handbooks

Companies often use the words "handbook" and "manual" interchangeably. Generally, an employee handbook is a document containing the policies of the company. Manuals generally contain procedures and are written for managers. Employment lawyers, management consultants, and managers disagree on the value and necessity for employee handbooks and procedure manuals, and some large companies do not use either.

One large Midwest company does not publish a policy manual. Instead, it uses a comprehensive communication process that starts with an orientation and follows up with internal newsletter articles, manager communication meetings, and company announcements. For its size, this company has been remarkably free from employee lawsuits. Most companies, however, use written guidelines because these provide a blueprint of where the company is going and the policies and procedures for how it will get there.

Most companies also give employees a simple guide or employee handbook that identifies what the firm expects of them at work. Relying on printed employee handbooks and procedure manuals reduces inconsistencies, errors, and poor judgment that may result in mistakes, wasted time and effort, grievances, and employee lawsuits.

Personnel Files

Human resource records have three major functions in a company. They may serve as (1) a memory or recall aid to managers and employees; (2) documentation of events for use in resolving questions or human resource problems; and (3) data for research, planning, problem solving, and decision making.

Federal, state, and local laws require that a variety of data on employees be maintained. However, even without such laws, it would be necessary to keep basic records to avoid errors of memory and to provide basic information to make management and human resource decisions. Managers need basic information on employee tenure and performance for review and decision making.

There are benefits to be derived from accurate and valid records. Good records permit managers to see how well the company is doing. Employee accomplishments and other critical events are documented. When there are queries about pay, disciplinary action, qualification, or experience, good documentation is essential. If a company uses good management and human resource practices, records are invaluable in defending against employee lawsuits and charges.

What Should Be in the File

The contents of human resource files vary by company size and industry, but some practices are accepted by most HR professionals. **Figure V-1** is a checklist of items that may be included in the official HR file. For example, there may be business reasons for filing all tuition reimbursements or wage assignments together. As a practical matter, most companies want the information in the employee's official HR file to be as complete as possible.

What Should Not Be in the Files

It is a poor management and human resource practice to file everything in the human resource files; however, many companies do not have a policy on the items that should be included in the official file and those that shouldn't. Many companies pay little attention to the contents of HR files until a problem occurs and the files are used as evidence of unlawful activity or discrimination. Consultants conducting assessments of HR departments routinely find problems and deficiencies in the contents of human resource files. These problems may include inappropriate documentation such as the following:

- Data identifying medical information, occupational injuries, and disabilities.
- Racial designations on self-identification documents for affirmative action purposes.
- Application forms that ask for and include non-job-related data.
- Subjective and inappropriate comments on performance appraisal forms.
- Immigration Control Form I-9.
- Poorly written and subjective documentation.
- Trivial, outdated, or nonessential performance comments.

Any medical information or information about the employee's physical condition must be kept strictly confidential, with access limited to those with a job-related need to know. Managers generally should not have access to any of this information unless a work accommodation is required.

The Immigration Reform and Control Act of 1986 requires employers to complete and have on file I-9 forms documenting employees' legal right to work in the United States. The I-9s should be filed separately from the official human resource file for at least two reasons. First, in completing the form, many employers make copies of the required identification documents and attach them to the form. At least one ID must have a photograph. Information showing the race or gender of an employee should not be in the official HR file. Second, during a compliance audit or investigation, auditors are empowered to refer evidence found in their investigation to other agencies such as the Immigration and Naturalization Service. Companies should avoid causing problems for themselves by making it easy to find violations.

Note: I-9 forms must be retained at the site of employment, although many companies forward copies to corporate headquarters.

Unofficial Files

Many supervisors and managers keep rough notes, copies of formal documents, and informal performance evaluations in department or their own private files. Two problems can arise from this practice. First, the company probably cannot monitor individual corrective action and informal discipline unless all documentation is filed in a single location. Second, a formal action might be revised or withdrawn; if there is a second, unofficial file, the company cannot be sure the copies have been destroyed. In resolving a charge or employee relations lawsuit, these informal files can be used as evidence.

Figure V-1. Suggested HR Files

MAIN EMPLOYEE FILE

>   Offer/transfer letter
>   Application form
>   W-4 form
>   Nondisclosure agreement
>   Software copyright compliance agreement
>   Orientation checklist
>   Termination checklist
>   Performance appraisals
>   Salary review
>   Official performance documentation (memos, letters, etc.)
>   Payroll documentation (e.g., change of address, cost center change, leave of absence, etc.)
>   Tuition aid requests
>   Copies of certificates, licenses, diplomas, etc.

SEPARATE MEDICAL/INSURANCE FILE

>   Group benefit enrollment forms
>   Profit-sharing, 401(k)/enrollment, change forms, etc.
>   Insurance claim forms
>   Consolidated Omnibus Budget Reconciliation Act letter sent

SUBJECT FILES KEPT SEPARATE
(usually in one folder for all affected employees; information kept in chronological order or by quarter)

>   Child support
>   EEO charges
>   Exit interview form
>   Garnishments
>   Immigration control form I-9—lawful employment
>   Litigation documents
>   Reference checks
>   Requests for employment/payroll verification
>   Wage assignments
>   Workers' compensation claims

SEPARATE PAYROLL FILES

>   Credit union deduction authorization
>   Savings on authorization

OTHER FILES

>   Targeted jobs tax credit forms
>   Minority status information

Records Retention

Records retention requirements are normally set by federal, state, and local laws or regulations. The annual *Guide to Federal Records Retention* details records retention requirements set by the federal government. State and local requirements vary; check with the local library or contact SHRM's Information Center for general information. Companies should contact local professionals, consultants, or an employee relations lawyer for more detailed information.

Files should be scrutinized periodically to expunge outdated or unnecessary information and documentation. Files of long-term employees may have information and data that were legal when prepared but that may be evidence of discrimination today. Many applications from 1950 through the late 1980s contain requests for information about race, marital status, parentage, children, spouses, and disabilities. The information required of current employees is limited to that which is job-related.

From a practical point of view, most companies retain basic employee records for the life of the company. After a certain time, these records are often filed in "dead storage" or encoded on storage tape.

Requirements for retention of employment applications differ depending on whether they are solicited or unsolicited. Unsolicited resumes and applications do not have to be retained at all, and many companies refuse to accept applications except when there are open positions. They return unsolicited resumes to the sender. Solicited applications and resumes of applications not hired should be maintained for at least six months, which is the length of time an applicant has to file a discrimination charge for failure to hire. Most companies keep applications for at least a year. Some companies have policies that define different retention periods for those interviewed and not interviewed.

The Equal Employment Opportunity Commission has advised that all resumes from online databases should be considered as solicited. They must be retained for at least the minimum time. These resumes must also be considered as candidates for purposes of calculating a company's applicant flow rate for minorities and females.

Employee Access to Records

Employees' rights to access to their own files is a dilemma with respect to employee interests and the right of the company to obtain, maintain, and use the employee's information. The human resource file often contains sensitive information from the application and preemployment screening process. In addition, the company has probably added data on performance, corrective action, readiness for promotion, and salary. Without access to their own files, employees cannot determine whether they have been treated fairly. Companies generally allow employees limited access to their own information.

The Privacy Act of 1974 guarantees federal employees the right to know the type of information collected on them, review the information, correct or have deleted any wrong information, and restrict access to their files. Although this law applies only to federal employees, some states have adopted strict regulations concerning access. According to a major survey, private employers have generally decided to allow employees to see their files. Procedures vary, but employees commonly have the right to view their files, to know what information is added, and to restrict the release of that information. They have access to preemployment documents, performance appraisals, salary records, and corrective action documentation. Some employers allow employees to copy information from their files and to correct or reply to information with which they disagree.

There are some benefits to allowing employees to view their human resource files. First, it allays their fears about what might be in their files, which is good for morale. Second, employers who know files may be viewed tend to be more careful about the type, format, and verification of the information, and it tends to be more objective.

Remember, having clear, well-written, objective documentation is essential when the information is used to defend a company against employee relations charges and discrimination lawsuits. The best source for this information should be the official human resource file.

Documentation

Every manager has to cope with one major problem: the inability of managers and supervisors to write clear, understandable, honest, and brief documentation. Clear writing of notes and formal comments of both praise and criticism are crucial for reliable and useful information for employee decision making. Some companies use forms to provide a guideline to ensure that all points are covered. Two sample forms are included at the end of this chapter, an Employee Counseling Form **(HRV-2.FRM)** and a Corrective Action Form **(HRV-3.FRM)**.

Human Resource Information Systems

Computer-based human resource information systems have grown in importance to the point where most companies cannot operate without them. A human resource information system (HRIS) is any system used to collect, store, maintain, retrieve, and administer information required by a company to manage its human resources. Most companies already use some computer programs to store data. Computer use ranges from payroll only to the storage and retrieval of applicant flow data for affirmative action compliance programs. The system includes a small mainframe to local area networks and generic software on individual personal computers. The resources available to help in the selection and implementation of an HRIS will determine whether it should be considered at the initial states of starting an HR function.

A good discussion of HRIS can be found in *Managing HR in the Information Age,* published by SHRM and Bureau of National Affairs. The chapter on HRIS lists some uses for a system (see **Figure V-2**).

Figure V-2. Uses of HRIS

Affirmative action/equal employment opportunity	Payroll
Applicant tracking	Pension administration
Attitude surveys	Productivity/work measurement
Benefits management	Project and event scheduling
Career planning and assessment	Safety and health
Employee history and records	Salary planning and administration
Human resource planning and forecasting	Succession planning
Job analysis	Tuition refund
Job evaluation	Turnover analysis
Labor relations	

Converting from a manual information system to an HRIS is a significant undertaking. It requires careful planning, and the decision should be made by the operating managers as well as human resource professionals. Management support is essential.

HRV-1.FRM

Sample Table of Contents
Employment Handbook

INTRODUCTION
- CEO Letter of Introduction
- Introduction to Company
- Company Mission
- Company History
- New Employee Orientation

EMPLOYMENT
- Employee Relations
- Equal Employment Opportunity
- Sexual Harassment
- Hiring of Relatives
- Employee Medical Examinations
- Immigration Law Compliance
- Conflict of Interest
- Disability Accommodation

EMPLOYMENT STATUS AND RECORD
- Employment Categories
- Access to Personnel Files
- Reference Checks
- Performance Management
- Job Descriptions

COMPENSATION AND BENEFITS
- Employee Benefits
- Time Off with Pay
- Holidays
- Health/Medical and Dental Insurance
- Life Insurance
- Cafeteria Section 125 Plan
- Workers' Compensation Insurance
- Time Off to Vote
- Jury Duty
- Savings Plan
- Credit Union
- Employee Assistance Plan (EAP)
- Salary Administration
- Promotions and Transfers
- Benefits Continuation (COBRA)

TIMEKEEPING/PAYROLL
- Timekeeping (Nonexempt)
- Paydays
- Employment Termination

WORKPLACE PROCEDURES
- Safety and Accident Prevention
- Smoking
- Overtime
- Special Situations (Nonexempt)
- Expense Reimbursement
- Vehicle Insurance — Official Business
- Moonlighting/Second Job
- Political Activity

LEAVE OF ABSENCE
- Family and Medical Leave
- Personal Leave
- Military Leave
- Funeral Leave

EMPLOYEE CONDUCT AND DISCIPLINARY ACTION
- Standards of Conduct and Discipline
- Progressive Discipline Guidelines
- Alcohol and Drug Use
- Sexual and Other Harassment
- Attendance and Punctuality
- Personal Appearance
- Company Property
- Restrictions on Solicitation
- Problem Resolution/Grievance Process

Employee Counseling Form

NAME: _____

JOB TITLE: _____   DEPARTMENT: _____

DATE OF INCIDENT: _____

DESCRIBE INCIDENT: _____

_____

_____

_____

_____

_____

_____

_____

_____

_____

_____

_____

_____

_____

_____

_____

_____

_____

EMPLOYEE COMMENTS: _____

_____

_____

_____

ACTION TAKEN   First warning ☐   Second warning ☐   Final warning ☐

You are given this notice so that you may have an opportunity to correct the problem. If the situation is repeated or if you engage in any other breach of our expectations, you will be subject to other appropriate corrective action.

Supervisor signature: _____   Date: _____

I have received a copy of this notice. I have read this notice and have had an opportunity to discuss it with my supervisor. I understand the rules and requirements.

Employee signature: _____   Date: _____

HRV-3.FRM

Corrective Action Form

NAME: _____

JOB TITLE: _____   DEPARTMENT: _____

DATE OF INCIDENT: _____

State the nature of the problem and the solution sought exactly as discussed with the employee.

_____

_____

_____

_____

_____

_____

_____

_____

_____

_____

Describe the activities required for improvement and the benchmarks.	Completion dates
_____	_____
_____	_____
_____	_____
_____	_____
_____	_____
_____	_____
_____	_____
_____	_____
_____	_____
_____	_____
_____	_____

EMPLOYEE COMMENTS: _____

_____

_____

_____

Supervisor signature: _____   Date: _____

I have received a copy of this notice. I have read this notice and have had an opportunity to discuss it with my supervisor. I understand the requirements and expectations.

Employee signature: _____   Date: _____

Chapter VI

Safety, OSHA, and Workers' Compensation

In many human resource departments, especially in small businesses, employee safety, Occupational Safety and Health Act (OSHA) compliance, and workers' compensation issues are not a key area of accountability. However, the mission of human resources involves the full use of employees, which requires a comprehensive approach and management commitment to ensuring a safe workplace. This chapter provides a historical review of employee safety and health and workers' compensation insurance, suggestions for starting a safety program, an outline of OSHA recordkeeping requirements, procedures for responding to accidents and injuries, and a case management process for early return to work.

Historical Review

Workers' compensation insurance programs are mandated by individual state laws. The purpose is to provide an injured employee the means to obtain medical attention and to provide reasonable compensation for the damage he or she has suffered because of being injured on the job. In the past, employers could reduce legal fees and limit their liability, because the system defined what was recoverable. However, in recent years, permanent partial disability awards have escalated dramatically, with carpal tunnel syndrome, hearing loss, and stress-related illnesses common. Businesses may also be the victims of employees with invalid claims.

In 1970, the federal government entered the safety arena with the Occupational Safety and Health Act. Under OSHA, employers are subject to the "general duty clause" and "general industry standards," which mandate that they provide a safe work environment.

In 1990, Congress passed the Americans with Disabilities Act (ADA), which protects qualified disabled persons from unlawful discrimination in employment, public services and transportation, public accommodations, and telecommunication services. This act affects how employee injuries are handled. An employer must make reasonable accommodations for persons with disabilities unless doing so would place undue hardship on the employer. Since ADA became the law, almost 70 percent of discrimination charges have been for failure to accommodate workers who have suffered occupational injuries.

Starting a Safety Program

Every accident has a cause. Once the cause is known, preventing future accidents is possible. Because each workplace is different, safety programs will also differ, but regardless of the size of a business, there are four requirements for preventing workplace accidents and injuries: (1) management commitment and employee involvement, (2) planning and organizing, (3) a safety committee, and (4) a worksite audit.

Management Commitment and Employee Involvement

To start a safety program, management must be informed about safety and have a positive attitude about maintaining a safe workplace. If management is unwilling to show its commitment (mainly by providing resources), no one else will be interested. Management must communicate and reinforce this commitment through the actions of all supervisors.

A manufacturing plant manager finds his reserved parking space occupied by another employee's vehicle. Instead of parking in another parking space, he parks his car in a fire lane. Many employees observe the safety violation; although it is minor, it clearly demonstrates how the manager feels about safety. This plant manager also routinely climbs over rail car couplings instead of walking around the end of the siding, another plant safety violation. These kinds of actions make the job of maintaining a safe workplace more difficult. They make disciplining someone for even a severe infraction almost impossible.

Planning and Organizing

As with any other business activity, safety and accident prevention require comprehensive planning by both management and employees. The strategic planning process for safety is similar to other management planning processes. Safety committee members are involved in ongoing strategy and planning, which includes an audit of the work environment, setting specific goals for improvement, delegating responsibility, and setting milestone and completion dates. Nowhere is the slogan "If you do not plan to succeed, you plan to fail" more true than in the area of safety.

The Safety Committee

Safety committees are essential to an effective safety effort; however, their effectiveness and value depend largely on how they are organized and managed. Safety committees should be designed to fill a specific need; for example, a small employer will likely have only one committee with a few members, while a large company will have a safety committee, maybe more than one, in each plant or facility.

There has been some confusion about safety committees and employee improvement teams. The National Labor Relations Board has found that certain "employee participation committee" activities may be illegal under the National Labor Relations Act of 1935. However, if management has a good understanding of the improvement team process, there should not be a problem. Employee participation committees, if designed properly, do not usurp the authority of the legally elected representatives of the employees. Safety committees can be beneficial, create a loyal and committed workforce, and lead to substantially increased productivity and quality. A few general rules apply to safety committees:

- Members of safety committees must not represent other employees.
- Safety committee deliberations must avoid discussions of financial rewards for safety improvement.
- Safety committees may assume management responsibilities such as safety inspections and accident investigations.
- Although employee safety is a management right, if employees are represented by a union, management should involve the union in the design and implementation of the safety committee.

Human resource professionals may want to discuss forming a safety committee with experienced employee relations professionals or HR consultants. The SHRM Information Center can provide reprints of articles written by employee relations specialists and labor lawyers about improvement teams and employee participation committees.

The safety committee should clearly explain that the sole objective of the committee is to prevent accidents. It should cover membership, terms, selection, responsibilities and accountabilities, specific duties, specific activities and functions, and overall authority. It is generally accepted that activity involving the safety of employees is not a subject of bargaining. Normally an employer can assert that management has reserved this right for itself. Be careful, however; many companies abdicate their right to use discretion in this area through past practice of not using it.

Management should appoint all members of any safety committee. Although safety committees can be composed of employees from each functional area, the members should not be described as representing a department or a group of employees.

Although the human resource person or another management official often functions as the committee chair, this is not a requirement. However, the chair should be a responsible person capable of running a meeting, setting priorities, and keeping committee activities at a high level. If the chair is not an experienced meeting facilitator (most managers and employees are not), he or she should receive training. The HR professional might consider being the chair, initially. After successful experiences with safety activities, a supervisor or hourly employee may be appointed. If possible, a maintenance engineer should be a member, to provide technical and equipment information that will help the committee make safety improvement decisions.

Some suggestions for functions of the safety committee are listed in **Figure VI-1**.

Figure VI-1. Safety Committee Functions

- Investigate serious or dangerous accidents.
- Conduct area safety inspections and observe employee work habits to detect unsafe acts.
- Monitor housekeeping levels and initiate corrective action.
- Review and evaluate protective equipment needs.
- Review the safety program and recommend improvement.
- Periodically review safety rules and recommend changes.
- Review and evaluate existing hazards and new installations with the intent to eliminate or reduce any known hazards.
- Send information gained in training sessions to all employees.
- Review accident and injury data on an ongoing basis.

A safety committee meeting may become a complaint session, in which a member brings up a safety problem and a management member is assigned to solve the problem. Management often requires too little of the hourly members of the committee. A second common problem is lack of training in problem solving, decision making, productivity improvement, and accident prevention techniques. Members rarely have a clear understanding of their role on the committee. Finally, companies often do not recognize committee participation, and other employees may perceive it as another useless committee with no benefit and no useful suggestions.

The Worksite Audit

A preliminary step in starting a safety program and meeting OSHA requirements is to conduct a worksite audit. This is a formal safety assessment to provide information about areas where safety activities are adequate, where they can be improved, and where they require immediate attention. The *OSHA Handbook for Small Businesses* contains a self-inspection format that can be adapted for use in different companies. As an alternative, the employer may want to retain a professional safety consultant or an HR professional for advice. (Choosing consultants and advisors is discussed in chapter IX.) Regardless of whether the company conducts its own audit or obtains outside advice, it has the responsibility to know what hazards are present in the workplace. Once the audit system is set up, conducting safety audits will be easy.

Figure VI-2 is a sample from a safety audit questionnaire (the entire questionnaire consists of 400 questions). Each question is assigned a weight. A summary report is provided to the client that tells where the company is strong and where it needs to improve safety activities.

Figure VI-2. Safety Audit Questionnaire

Do you have an accident investigation procedure?

Does the procedure require that injuries, occupational illnesses, property damage, accidents, and near misses be reported?

Does it require training supervisors in investigation and reporting?

Is there a standard form for accident investigation?

Do employees participate in accident investigations?

Is the atmosphere one of fact finding rather than fault finding?

Does your accident investigation program require
   a. a complete investigation by the immediate supervisor, with the results recorded on a standard form?
   b. that injury and alleged causal information on all injuries treated by first aid be recorded?
   c. that serious accidents and near misses be called to the attention of the group manager to ensure full investigation?

Figure VI-2. Safety Audit Questionnaire (continued)

Is a monthly check made of the following areas to learn the number of accidents reported?

    a. first aid stations and medical treatment center.

    b. maintenance shops, storerooms, and equipment storage areas.

    c. fire control center.

Is there a procedure for ensuring that remedial action (and follow-up of that action) as recommended in the investigation report is carried out?

Do you have an organized system to ensure that all remedial action listed on major loss accidents has been taken? If yes, does it include

    a. a periodic report from the area supervisor on the status of incomplete remedial actions?

    b. follow-up by the appropriate person, with item-by-item checkoff as actions are completed?

How frequently is management made aware of the progress of remedial action taken on major or high-potential-loss accidents?

Is the progress of remedial action expressed in written form?

Is it also expressed orally at meetings?

Are summaries of the vital information on major injuries or illnesses written and distributed to department managers within 24 hours of the occurrence?

Are summaries of major property damage accidents and fires written and distributed to department heads within 48 hours of the occurrence?

Are the considerations and declarations of investigation review meetings recorded?

How often is an audit made of the percentage of accidents investigated?

Are the findings communicated in written form to all managers?

Is there a system to evaluate the quality of accident investigation reports?

How often is this done and recorded?

Are these evaluations communicated to all levels of management?

Safety Inspections

Inspections are the main tools for detecting unsafe conditions. Regular safety inspections ferret out unsafe conditions. There are two kinds of safety inspections, the incidental inspection and the planned inspection.

Incidental inspections

The incidental inspection is largely a matter of keeping your eyes open. Most supervisors inspect their areas this way. Such inspections are useful, but they are usually superficial and erratic. When supervisors become engrossed in other matters, incidental inspection virtually ceases.

Planned inspections

The planned inspection is deliberate and thorough. The supervisor knows the area and knows what tools, equipment, machines, etc., require inspection. There is a checklist for recording inspection items and findings. Inspection of this kind does not leave anything to chance. Unsafe conditions are much more likely to be spotted.

To initiate safety inspections, one must first conduct a safety inspection inventory to ascertain, for example, who is responsible for what areas, what items in each area require regular inspection, what conditions should be checked, how frequently the items should be inspected, who should inspect the items, and which items require special equipment and techniques for inspection.

Most companies develop a list of the tools, equipment, machines, structures, supplies, etc. that require regular inspection, based on knowledge of unsafe conditions that have occurred in the past. When a tool, machine, structure, or piece of equipment is inspected, attention should be paid to the parts that can create unsafe conditions. The employer should decide exactly what parts of each tool should be inspected regularly. **Figure VI-3** lists a number of ideas for developing a safety inspection inventory.

Figure VI-3. Safety Inspection Inventory

Atmospheric conditions: dusts, gases, fumes, sprays, illumination
Buildings and structures: windows, doors, floors, stairs, roofs, walls
Containers: scrap bins, disposal receptacles, barrels, carboys, gas cylinders, solvent cans
Electrical equipment: switches, cables, outlets, connectors, grounds, connections
Elevators, escalators, and lifts: cable, controls, safety devices
Firefighting equipment: extinguishers, hoses, hydrants, sprinkler systems, alarms
Hand tools: bars, sledges, wrenches, hammers; also, power hand tools
Hazardous supplies and materials: flammables, explosives, acids, caustics, toxic chemicals
Material handling equipment: conveyors, cranes, hoists, forklifts
Personal protective equipment: hardhats, safety glasses, respirators, gas masks
Pressurized equipment: boilers, vats, tanks, piping, hosing
Production and related equipment: Any equipment that processes materials into more finished products, e.g., mills, shapers, cutters, borers, presses, lathes
Personnel supporting equipment: ladders, scaffolding, high platforms, catwalks, sling chairs, staging
Power source equipment: gas engines, steam engines, electrical motors
Structural openings: shafts, pits, sumps, and floor openings, including those usually kept covered
Storage facilities and areas: racks, bins, cabinets, shelves, tanks, closets; also, yard and floor storage areas
Transportation equipment: automobiles, trucks, railroad cars, motorized carts, buggies
Walkways and roadways: aisles, ramps, docks, walkways, vehicle ways
Warning and signaling devices: crossing lights, blinker lights, sirens, claxons, warning signs
Miscellaneous: items that do not fall into any of the above categories

The person conducting an inspection relies mainly on his or her knowledge and experience to decide what to inspect. Other sources of ideas include equipment operators, other supervisors, safety personnel, manufacturer equipment manuals, and accident records. The National Safety Council's *Handbook for Industrial Operations* is an excellent source of inspection ideas.

Safety

OSHA requires that all employees be trained for safety in specific areas. Employees also need education on the technical aspects of the job and on safety topics. Employers must provide and document OSHA-required training to avoid being cited and fined. If technical, job-specific training is not provided, employees will not know how to avoid accidents. If education on safety topics is not provided, employees will not have the basic skills to identify hazards and avoid injury.

When an employee moves into a new position, the employer should provide an orientation on safety as it relates to that position. The object of the orientation should be to acquaint the employee with safety matters specifically related to the activities of the new position. The areas listed in **Figure VI-4** can be used to develop a safety orientation process.

Figure VI-4. Safety Orientation

- **Major area hazards.** Explain any major area hazards the new employee will be exposed to and what precautions are expected.

- **Personal protective equipment.** Protective equipment should be issued to the employee, and its use explained.

- **Housekeeping and clean-up responsibilities.** Acquaint the employee with his or her housekeeping and clean-up responsibilities. Poor housekeeping is a major cause of accidents and injuries; employee responsibility for housekeeping should be clearly defined.

- **Critical safety rules.** Safety rules should be explained immediately.

Many supervisors mistakenly think they are giving pre-job safety instruction when they urge employees to be careful before sending them on their way. To do any good, pre-job safety instructions must be specific to the concerns listed in **Figure VI-5**.

Figure VI-5. Pre-Job Safety Instructions

- **Potential accidents.** Possibilities of fire, explosion, toxic gases, electrical contacts, chemical contacts, cave-ins, falls, or other potentially serious accidents should be discussed, and precautions agreed upon.

- **Unsafe practices.** Some jobs may tempt employees into unsafe practices, e.g., throwing materials down instead of lowering them, failing to lock out equipment, and neglecting to rope off areas.

- **Protective equipment.** When jobs require special protective equipment, the assigning supervisor should see to it that the employees get the equipment.

- **"Other-fellow" precautions.** Many repair, service, and construction jobs require special precautions be taken to protect workers in the area.

Effective job safety training is a never-ending communication to employees of safety matters, i.e., hazards, safety rules, safe job procedures, accident causes, etc.

Pre-job safety instructions rarely take more than five minutes. That is a small price to pay to avoid a crippling or fatal injury or accident.

Recordkeeping Requirements

OSHA requires employers to keep certain records, to gather and store information about accidents. These facts often identify causes, and OSHA can begin control procedures to prevent similar accidents. OSHA requirements are listed in **Figure VI-6**.

Figure VI-6. OSHA Recordkeeping Requirements

- Obtain a report on every injury requiring medical treatment (death, disabling, or medical aid).

- Record each injury on OSHA Form 200 according to the instructions provided.

- Prepare a supplementary record of occupational injuries and illnesses for recordable cases either on OSHA Form 101 or on State Employers First Report of Injury.

- Every year, prepare the annual summary (OSHA Form 200); post it by February 1, and keep it posted until March 1. Posting it next to the OSHA workplace poster and the business safety policy is a good idea.

- Certain OSHA standards that deal with toxic substances and hazardous exposures require records on the exposure of employees, physical examination reports, employment records, etc. As you identify hazards, you can decide whether these requirements apply to your situation on a case-by-case basis.

- Although OSHA requires that employers retain these records for at least five years, most companies keep them for the life of the business.

OSHA forms are available from the Government Printing Office and from state and local departments of labor (through their occupational safety and health administrations).

These requirements may seem onerous, but they are the minimum. During the year, the records should be reviewed to see where injuries are occurring and to identify high-exposure and high-risk areas to which attention should be directed. These basic OSHA records include only injury and illness cases. They should be expanded to include data that can pinpoint unsafe conditions or procedures. Other reports will be discussed later.

The Department of Labor (DOL) Bureau of Labor Statistics publishes *Recordkeeping Guidelines for Occupational Injuries and Illnesses*, which includes complete information for recordkeeping required by OSHA. Only two forms are used for OSHA recordkeeping. OSHA Form 200 serves two purposes: It is the Log of Occupational Injuries and Illnesses on which to record the occurrence, extent, and outcomes of cases and also the Summary of Occupational Injuries and Illnesses, which is used to summarize the log at the end of the year. This summary must be posted in February.

OSHA Form 101, Supplementary Record of Occupational Injuries and Illnesses, provides additional information on each of the recorded cases. These forms are available from DOL and OSHA. The information gathered can also be useful in tracking improvement. OSHA Form 200 asks the employer to calculate lost time (or disabling) rate, severity rate, and medical aid (or recordable) rate, which is also generally considered the accident incident rate.

Accident Investigations

Many employers use the First Report of Injury required by state workers' compensation systems as the sole accident investigation form. A better form is provided at the end of this chapter (**HRVI-1.FRM**); employers can revise it for their specific needs. Most companies with successful accident and injury prevention programs use a comprehensive form. A similar form is available from the National Safety Council.

The workers' compensation system normally limits awards for occupational injuries and illnesses; thus, the employer is strictly liable and fault does not enter the process. However, a comprehensive accident investigation must identify specific causes and inquire into what employees either did or failed to do that caused the accident or injury. This report requires detailed, precise data, which may find the employer negligent in not preventing the accident. If there is additional litigation outside the workers' compensation area, the accident investigation report may be discoverable by opposing counsel. However, without comprehensive accident investigation documentation, injuries and accidents will never be reduced.

The ultimate purpose of an accident investigation is to collect information that can be used to prevent a recurrence of the accident. The investigation should seek to answer these questions:

- Who experienced the accident?
- When did the accident occur?
- Where did the accident occur?
- What position was being worked?
- What job was being done?
- What occurred?
- What where the causes of the accident?
- How can recurrence be prevented?

Two important issues in accident investigation are (1) reluctance to acknowledge responsibility and (2) lack of proper concern for minor accidents. Supervisors who are nominally responsible for accidents are often reluctant to acknowledge accident causes that reflect on their own indifference, lack of action, or other contributing responsibility. Supervisors may investigate accidents with a defensive attitude and a readiness to blame the employee involved. A practical solution is to have injury accidents analyzed by an investigating committee consisting of one or more neutral supervisors plus the supervisor who is nominally responsible. Many companies use their safety committees for accident investigation. These committees usually conduct more thorough investigations than an individual investigator does.

There is often an understandable, but mistaken, lack of concern for minor accidents. Supervisors who tolerate superficial investigations of minor injury accidents show a poor attitude toward safety. A supervisor's lack of concern for injury prevention teaches employees that they do not have to be concerned about their own safety and that conditions that cause injuries do not have to be corrected.

For information on accident investigation, contact the National Safety Council or a safety practitioner or consultant.

Accident investigation reports usually are reviewed and filed. Sometimes they are discussed in management staff meetings and safety committee meetings. Occasionally, mechanical or engineering issues are identified and repairs and modifications made. Seldom are the reports used to their full potential.

The report form below (**Figure VI-7**) lists critical items that can be extracted from the accident report to calculate the type, number, and causes of injuries. This form provides ongoing information about where accidents and injuries occur and their causes. Workers' compensation insurance carriers have loss prevention departments that are supposed to provide assistance in reducing accidents; however, they often use reports that are not very detailed, and they do not summarize injuries and accidents annually. Most companies require more timely data.

A multilocation construction employer requested help with its safety efforts, specifically on required recordkeeping for multiple locations and how to use the data. The employer was part of a "risk pool," in which several companies had joined together to purchase workers' compensation insurance as a group. This usually results in lower premiums; however, if one member of the pool has a high claims experience, the other members share the increased cost. Accurate accident and injury information is essential for this arrangement to work, but this company had only its own first report of injuries and the workers' compensation insurance administrator's loss control data.

Figure VI-7. Cumulative Accident Report Form

Body Parts Analysis—1995

Month	Head	Eyes	Neck	Back	L/arm	L/hand	Fingers	R/arm	R/hand	L/leg	L/foot	R/leg	R/foot
January													
February													
March													
April													
May													
Totals													

Contributing Factors—1995

Month	Unaware of job hazards	Inattentive to hazards	Unaware of safe methods	Low level of skill	Saving time	Avoiding extra effort
January						
February						
March						
April						
May						

From this small amount of data, information was reconstructed to support safety improvement recommendations. First, from the loss data, accident incidence and severity rates were calculated for each location, as shown in **Figure VI-8**. (The model form [HRVI-2.FRM] included at the end of this chapter can be used for a single location.) It was apparent where the problem with accidents and injuries existed. Although not shown here, the severity rate (the number of days lost to injuries per 200,000 hours worked) also was calculated. This calculation can identify serious hazards. However, the difference between the significance of a first-aid or near-miss accident and a serious disabling injury is slight. Most safety professionals strongly believe that for every serious injury, the injured employee has done the same thing, the same way, and not been injured. Successful safety and injury prevention programs focus as much on near-miss incidents as they do on exposure to serious, possibly disabling injuries.

Figure VI-8. Accident Loss Data, by Location

Location	Hours 1993	Lost Time Cases	Lost Time Rate*	Medical Aid Cases	Medical Aid Rate*	First Aid Cases	Priority
Phoenix, AZ	xxx,xxx,xxx	20	8.00	31	12.4	35	Third
San Francisco, CA	xxx,xxx,xxx	12	4.80	15	6	20	
Los Angeles, CA	xxx,xxx,xxx	11	4.40	17	6.8	19	
Colorado Springs, CO	xxx,xxx,xxx	31	12.40	45	18	59	First
Kansas City, MO	xxx,xxx,xxx	30	12.00	34	13.6	39	Second
Overland Park, KS	xxx,xxx,xxx	8	3.20	10	4	8	
St. Louis, MO	xxx,xxx,xxx	6	2.40	19	7.6	40	
Minneapolis, MN	xxx,xxx,xxx	7	2.80	23	9.2	36	
Omaha, NE	xxx,xxx,xxx	5	2.00	10	4	17	
Springfield, MO	xxx,xxx,xxx	7	2.80	11	4.4	20	
Las Vegas, NV	xxx,xxx,xxx	15	6.00	11	4.4	23	

Case Management

Sometimes, even with all the employer's efforts and preventive measures, someone is injured. What happens when an accident occurs? Since the passage of ADA in 1990, there has been some movement toward bringing injured employees back to work as soon as possible; in fact, refusal to bring a permanent partially disabled employee back to work may be a violation of ADA. But under the Family and Medical Leave Act of 1993 (FMLA), a partially disabled or injured employee cannot be forced to return to work on "light duty" before 12 weeks have elapsed. Numerous studies have shown that the sooner an injured employee returns to work (either to full duty or to an accommodated position), the more likely the employee is to return to full productivity. Conversely, if an employee is off work more than several weeks, the outlook for returning to full efficiency is diminished significantly. This issue is of significant concern for HR professionals.

Many employers use an internal case management process. Case management is the immediate review of any occupational injury requiring medical attention with the objective of reducing unnecessary medical cost, time lost from work, and permanent partial disability expenses.

Steve, a maintenance employee, inadvertently puts his forefinger into a conveyor drive chain and the tip is cut off. Instead of having a co-worker take Steve to the hospital, the manager, Loretta, accompanies him to the emergency room, to comfort Steve and to get firsthand information on what occurred. The emergency room physician sutures the severed fingertip and prescribes medication. Steve and Loretta discuss with the doctor the treatment, possible therapy, and prohibitions on returning to full duty. Steve and Loretta agree, and the physician concurs, that Steve should stay in the shop, performing benchwork for the next week. After the next doctor's appointment, Steve and Loretta will discuss any temporary disability and plan his return to full duty.

Both return to the plant, and while Loretta completes the accident investigation report, Steve gathers benchwork that has backed up and starts full-valued work. The total cost of this accident is less than $500, including the indirect cost of the manager's time at the emergency room.

In another organization, the scenario may have been different. Steve would be taken to the emergency room by a co-worker. Without a manager to discuss his return to work on light duty, Steve might be given a week off to recuperate. Loretta may have been busy and not have completed the accident investigation report for a few days. Steve would be missed on the job, but since he had a doctor's excuse, the time off would not have been questioned. At the very least, there would be no discussion until the doctor returned Steve to full duty. The direct costs (medical and temporary partial disability) could easily have exceeded $5,000; the indirect costs, twice that.

This simple case study illustrates how a proactive response to an accident can save a significant amount of money. Even more important since the passage of ADA is the result when there is a permanent partial disability and the employee cannot meet the full requirements of the job. As discussed previously, ADA requires employers to accommodate disability unless there is a business necessity. This law applies to hiring, but the largest number of complaints under ADA have been against employers who refuse to accommodate disabilities resulting from occupational injuries.

The issue of safety, workers' compensation, and ADA is too complicated to discuss fully here; however, the following factors should be considered in starting a safety program:

- The employer must have a policy on early return to work and adapting to the permanent disabilities of employees who are injured while working.
- ADA does not require job descriptions, but every position should be analyzed so that only the essential job functions are included as job requirements.
- Managers must receive a comprehensive education on safety, early return to work, and ADA issues. If managers do not understand the requirements and are not committed to the process, it will fail. Many discrimination charges have been filed against companies for ADA misjudgment.
- All employees must be given an orientation to the early return to work process. The objectives and process must be clearly understood by all.
- Managers' performance evaluations should be partially based on how well they reduce the number of injuries and accidents, comply with ADA, and manage the case management process.
- Human resource professionals should regularly monitor accident and injury reports and identify areas where employees are not returned to work immediately after an occupational injury.

Case management is not a fully developed process in most companies, but many consultants offer case management services. The most successful case management processes are those that require the manager and line supervisor to participate. This is especially true when considering ADA and FMLA issues. Only persons very familiar with the operations and work culture should be making decisions about whether the employer can adapt a position to a particular employee's temporary partial disability.

The chart in **Figure VI-9** is a model for a case management process.

Figure VI-9. The Case Management Process

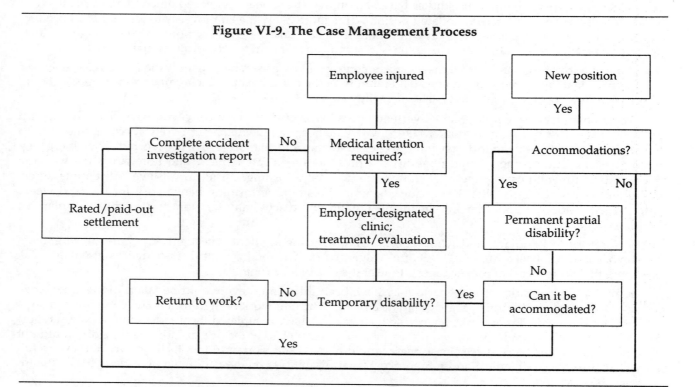

Employee safety is a major management function. Even without OSHA requirements, accidents and injuries not only cause employees pain and suffering, but cost the employer significantly more than just the workers' compensation insurance. The National Safety Council estimates the indirect costs of injuries and accidents—such as product and equipment damage, management investigation and reports, customer order delays, and co-worker inefficiencies—at more than 12 times the direct costs. Having a good safety and accident prevention program can be the key to remaining profitable.

Accident Investigation Form

PERSONAL INFORMATION

Name:		Employee no.	Age:	
Location:		Department:		
Time of accident:	Date of accident:	Date injury reported:	Date lost time started:	Date returned to work:
Position title:		Years of experience:	Specific activity being performed:	

Nature of injuries and injured body parts:

ACCIDENT DESCRIPTION AND RELATED INFORMATION

Exact location where accident occurred:

Job employee was doing at the time injured:

Describe exactly what occurred:

ANALYSIS OF ACCIDENT CAUSES

What did the injured (or other person) do or fail to do that contributed directly to the accident? Be specific.

Check the items below judged to be responsible for what was done or not done, thereby contributing to the accident. More than one may apply.
Write in any information or indirect causes not listed.

- Unaware of job hazards
- Inattentive to hazards
- Unaware of safe method
- Low level of job skill
- Tried to gain or save time
- Tried to avoid extra effort
- Acted to avoid discomfort

- Indirect cause(s) other than those listed

- Influence of emotions
- Influence of fatigue
- Influence of illness
- Influence of intoxicants
- Defective vision
- Defective hearing
- Other personal handicap

- Unable to judge nature of indirect causes

What defective or otherwise unsafe condition(s) of tools, equipment, machinery, structures, work area, etc., contributed to the accident?

Accident Investigation Form, p.2

Check the items below judged responsible for the development or existence of any defective or otherwise unsafe conditions that contributed to the accident. Check all conditions that apply. Write in the information for indirect causes not listed.

• Worn out from normal use	• Unsafe design
• Abuse or misuse by user(s)	• Faulty construction
• Overlooked by regular inspections	• Inadequate illumination
• Regular inspections not required	• Lubrication failure
• Housekeeping or clean-up failure	• Exposure to corrosion/rust
• Regular clean-up not required	• Exposure to vibration
• Inadequate ventilation	• Exposure to extreme temperature
• Congestion—lack of space	• Tampering; unauthorized removal
• Indirect cause(s) not listed above	• Unable to judge cause of contributing condition

ACTIONS TO PREVENT ACCIDENT RECURRENCE

Mark the corrective actions planned or already taken to prevent accident recurrence at the time of this report. More than one item may apply.

• Reinstruct employees involved	• Revise job safety analysis
• Reprimand persons involved	• Equipment repair or replacement
• Discipline persons involved	• Action to improve design
• Reinstruct others doing job	• Action to improve construction
• Temporary reassignment of person	• Installation of guard or safety device
• Permanent reassignment of person	• Correction of unnecessary congestion
• Action to improve inspection	• Improve personnel protective equipment
• Action to improve housekeeping	• Start new pre-job instruction
• Order job safety analysis conducted	• Use other materials
	• Communicate safety concern

• Other than above--please specify:

Describe details of any primary corrective action for disabling-injury or near-disabling-injury accidents.

Recommend any corrective actions needed to prevent accident recurrences that are beyond your authority to implement. Describe the basic idea.

MISCELLANEOUS INFORMATION

Names of witnesses:

Was a job safety analysis conducted? • yes • no		Was revision ordered? • yes • no

Investigated by:	Reviewed by:
Date:	Date:

HRVI-2.FRM

Accident/Injury Analysis Summary

	Hours Worked YTD/ Month	Total for month of					Year to date:				
		Lost Time Cases	Lost Time Rate *	Medical Aid Cases	Medical Aid Rate*	First Aid Cases	Lost Time Cases	Lost Time Rate *	Medical Aid Cases	Medical Aid Rate*	First Aid Cases
Maintenance											
Packaging											
Processing											
Materials handling											
Administration (includes all management/supervision)											
Total facility											

* Calculations:

Lost Time Rate (LTR)

$$\frac{\text{\# of lost time cases} \times 200{,}000 \text{ hours}}{\text{\# of hours worked}} = \text{LTR}$$

Medical Aid Rate (MAR)

$$\frac{\text{\# of medical cases} \times 200{,}000 \text{ hours}}{\text{\# of hours worked}} = \text{MAR}$$

Severity Rate (SR)

$$\frac{\text{\# of days lost} \times 200{,}000 \text{ hours}}{\text{\# of hours worked}} = \text{SR}$$

CHAPTER VII

TRAINING AND DEVELOPMENT

Employee development is anything that prepares employees to do their jobs better. This includes improving their skill levels and encouraging them to work toward common and mutually agreeable objectives. Company development focuses all of the company resources, including employee activities, toward working well together in a productive and motivational work environment; it is an ongoing effort to enhance the problemsolving, decision-making, and renewal process.

Failure to Train Is a Failure to Manage

Several years ago, a governor faced with a troubled prison system was asked what he planned to do to end the problem. "We are never going to have better prisons," he replied, "until we get a better quality of prisoners." When it comes to training, many managers have the same attitude. "Give us better workers," they say, "and all our problems will go away." Yet U.S. employers already have good workers. It takes effort to get any employee up to speed; it takes even more effort to develop a workforce that operates together like a well-oiled and well-maintained piece of equipment.

It is the company's responsibility to get employees from entry level to a level that meets or exceeds minimum standards. It does not matter if the new hires are Harvard MBAs, experienced employees hired from competitors, recent college graduates, or high-potential professionals enticed away from another industry. New hires are incompetent until they know the company's policies, procedures, systems, and culture. Once the employee is up to speed and can perform, the formal training process starts.

Many employers assume that employees have all the skills they need when they join the company, but this is seldom the case. Many managers do not have the knowledge or skills to train; consequently, they avoid the responsibility. Successful companies take this responsibility seriously and do not allow managers to avoid it.

Many employers understand the need for training for both their employees and management. So they call a consultant or a seminar company and announce that all supervisors will attend classes on meeting effectiveness, leadership, motivation, and delegation skills. Employees are scheduled for classes on quality and customer service. Everyone attends. Two years later, the problems remain. A few employees and supervisors have improved, but overall, the training was a waste of money. Usually, it is not the fault of the vendors. Consultants and seminar presenters can deliver only what the company asks for. No matter how excellent these programs, if the lack of a certain skill is not the problem, training is not the solution.

Employers who train employees in "people skills" or organizational development are repeating the mistakes that were made 30 years ago. In the 1960s, employers offered "sensitivity training" to improve company productivity. The intent of these sessions was to help employees become open to new ideas and become better listeners. Today, employees take seminars on diversity, team building, and communication. As they did 30 years ago, they leave the seminar and return to the same company culture, reward system, and management style they left. The newly trained employees, even if they want to change the way they do things, are faced with a company that believes "If it ain't broke, don't fix it."

For employees who need additional skills, an ongoing training process can improve individual employee productivity, but the process must augment activities required in the employer's strategic plan and must be based on employees' assessment of their own needs.

Training on Government Regulations

The Civil Rights Act of 1964. This law does not specifically require training, but it does hold the company and its managers responsible for acts of discrimination. Most employers offer training to managers and supervisors to make them aware of the issues involved and thus reduce the company's exposure to charges of discrimination and employee lawsuits.

Title VII of the Civil Rights Act prohibits sexual harassment in the workplace. The act does not specifically require training, but a U.S. Supreme Court decision held that an employer would be strictly liable for any sexual harassment. Training supervisors in what constitutes sexual harassment and how to deal with the issue lessens the liability. All employees must be told of the employer's policy against sexual harassment and how to use company procedures to file a complaint or grievance.

Affirmative action compliance. Executive Order 11246 requires federal contractors to train their supervisors and managers in the concepts of equal employment opportunity and to communicate the company's policy regularly in staff meetings and in company publications.

National Labor Relations Act. Most employers provide managers and supervisors with some training on employee relations. In unionized companies, most supervisors are trained in the administration of the union contract. In union-free companies, managers and supervisors are usually given significant training in human relations skills. Many union-free companies also provide specialized education in how to deal with organizing attempts.

OSHA–mandated training. Safety training is discussed in detail in chapter VI. OSHA has mandated general safety practices, hazard communication education, and employee training in the use and storage of potentially dangerous materials such as blood-born pathogens.

Employee Development

Training programs aimed at familiarizing employees with their jobs and improving their skills will help solve four problems: (1) ignorance about the mission and organization of the employer (why the company exists and how it satisfies the client); (2) confusion about what is to be accomplished on the job; (3) lack of sufficient job skills; and (4) lack of desire to perform (because they have not been recognized or rewarded in the past). Generally, the supervisor and employee should agree on the areas needing attention and select specific training that addresses these areas.

Use caution in identifying training needs without obtaining real agreement with the employee. A senior engineer in a city government had significant contact with the public, other departments, and the city council. The city manager's office had received many complaints about the engineer's inability to communicate effectively.

The engineering manager and the human resource director decided to send the engineer to a retreat in which participants evaluated their own and each other's communication skills. The retreat had no effect on the engineer's behavior; in fact, he was adamant about not having a communication problem. Much later, the engineering manager discovered that the engineer had perceived his training experience as punishment. Normally, the department budget included funds for attending a week-long engineering and planning conference; those resources were used to send the engineer to the training, which he did not believe he needed. Training must be mutually agreed upon, with a full understanding of the expectations.

Employee development focuses on self-awareness, motivation, and job skills. Companies typically seek to improve employee attitudes, behaviors, and accomplishments using the following processes:

- **Career development.** These programs help employees become more aware of their own interests and abilities. By helping employees think about a career rather than just a job, the employer can help them see their current job as a learning experience.

- **Personal assessment.** These programs are designed to help employees understand their strengths and the areas in which they need to improve. If employees accurately assess themselves and compare that assessment with the needs of the job, they have a better chance of doing well. These programs should be tied to the performance evaluation process.

- **Job skills programs.** These programs are oriented toward improving the technical skills of employees. On-the-job training (OJT) is the primary vehicle for initial job training. Formal OJT programs can make a significant impact on both the profitability of the employer and its ability to maintain a positive work environment, but much training is informal, with few guidelines or measurements of achievement. Informal processes seldom do more than get new employees up to a low level of achievement and may allow them to develop bad habits. In more successful formal training processes, employees participate in the planning, development, implementation, and, in many cases, administration of training. When both employees and supervisors are included, the program is usually effective and accepted.

Organizational Effectiveness Training

Training often is not tied to the employer's strategic plan; as a result, employees are given tools they cannot use. For example, communication and people skills are popular topics of training. However, employees cannot practice these skills if barriers exist such as lack of rewards and recognition, lack of information, or autocratic management.

Typically, training is scheduled individually; rarely is an entire work group trained together. Often, what an employee learns cannot be discussed with co-workers until they are trained, perhaps weeks or months later. If the interactions between manager and subordinates or among peers are to change, they must be in the classroom together.

There is a natural resistance to change, but employees do not resist all change. They do not resist salary increases. They do not resist improvements in their work environment. They resist changes they don't understand or that they believe might be to their disadvantage. Several classic studies show that employees do not resist change when they participate in the decision. When the employees participated in making job-related changes, they showed a rapid and sustained improvement in productivity. This basic theory is behind work teams and self-managed teams. If employers want to make workplace changes, they must find ways to (1) involve employees in decisions that affect their jobs, (2) develop open communications, and (3) build trust between workers and management.

Group-Oriented Training Process

The group-oriented training process is a well-accepted approach founded on group problem solving methodology. Following is an outline of the process.

Training the Committee

An education or training steering committee, usually composed of the top management team, is trained in group problemsolving methodology and provided with instruction in basic team improvement decision-making tools. An overview is presented of the scientific approach to improvement and the use of tools such as flowcharts, cause-and-effect diagrams, and check sheets.

Conducting an Assessment

An assessment must be made to ascertain the actual training needs. Picking courses from a seminar brochure or even asking employees what training they need is not effective. The committee should conduct a comprehensive assessment that might include a summary of performance appraisals, interviews with managers, and the results of an employee survey.

Selecting Pilot Training Projects

The committee uses a group decision-making tool to prioritize training and educational needs. Most facilitators prefer the nominal group technique that incorporates brainstorming, initial selection, and ranking. Then the committee chooses a pilot project or projects, depending on the number of crucial training needs and the resources available.

Expanding the Committee

Often the needs assessment reveals education or training requirements that would be better addressed at the department or a lower level. Training committees within those departments, or cross-functional committees, should be selected and trained, and the problems delegated to those committees. The original management training committee then becomes a steering committee, to which the other committees will report.

Conducting the Training and Evaluating the Results

After the pilot training project has been developed and conducted, the committee should evaluate its quality and usefulness. Although many employers use simple appraisal instruments, there are more efficient ways of showing a return on the investment. See the *Handbook of Training Evaluation and Measurement Methods, Developing Human Resources—Volume 5* (SHRM BNA Series), and *Forecasting Financial Benefits of Human Resource Development*. These books are listed in appendix A.

Special Training

Total Quality Management, Customer Service, and Team Building

These kinds of training are often offered generically, in one-size-fits-all sessions. However, employees and supervisors seldom control the resources required to provide quality or excellence in customer service. The culture of the employer must support these activities. The best models of quality transformation can be found in the stories of some of the stars of customer service. Several of the books listed in appendix A describe how these employers recognized the value of their employees and linked training to company objectives.

Management, Supervisor, and Leadership Training

Figure VII-1 lists some typical topics included in management and supervisor training programs.

Figure VII-1. Management and Supervisor Training Topics

- Transition to supervisor—Change focus from "doing" to "getting things done through others."
- Role of supervisor—Learn what supervisors really do.
- Administration of employer policies—Lessen misunderstanding of policies and reduce employee complaints and problems.
- Interviewing/selection—Hire better, more productive employees while reducing exposure to discrimination complaints.
- Conducting performance appraisals—Improve communication and coaching skills to develop better, more committed employees.
- Discipline and documentation—Correct unacceptable behavior fairly and efficiently.
- Team building—Build cooperation by teaching techniques of working together.
- Productivity improvement—Get more accomplished with less.
- Effective communications—Learn conversation and listening skills.
- Time management—Get things done on time.
- Effective decision making—Learn techniques for making the right decision at the right time.
- Supervisor as a trainer—Learn methods of instructing others to do things the right way.
- Evaluating performance—Institute effective ways to evaluate employees.
- Motivating employees—Learn practical patterns of employee behavior and how to get employees to do their best.

Too often employers provide supervisor and management training sporadically and without any real plan. Supervisors are sent to a seminar where they learn valuable information. Returning to a work environment where these new skills are not valued or reinforced, the supervisor soon reverts to the old way of doing things. Or employees may attend "feel-good, pop psychology" training conducted by well-known presenters. They come back energized, but again, with no reinforcement, there is no lasting improvement.

A consultant describes a firm in which he once worked. One department head was extremely autocratic, domineering, and controlling, which resulted in constant employee complaints and a 150 percent turnover in the professional staff over two years. The department was suffering from a lack of leadership, demoralized employees, and disgruntled clients. The managing partner asked an industrial psychologist for assistance, and she suggested a needs assessment process in which subordinates and peers would evaluate the department head's management style, identifying their perception of his strengths and weaknesses. The boss would then attend a week-long retreat where a performance improvement plan would be developed.

All went as planned, even though the department head carefully selected those who would evaluate him, choosing people he thought would be positive about his management style. The comments were extremely critical and he was not pleased. However, to his credit, he vowed to change. And he did try.

But the culture of the firm was focused on the short term and the bottom line, with performance based solely on financial measurements and sales goals. There was no margin for communicating with subordinates and no budget for developing teamwork. The pressure was continuous to make the department profitable right now. There was no incentive to change the dysfunctional behaviors that were causing problems in the department. Three months later, when the evaluation instrument was distributed again, the response showed that not only was there no improvement, the boss's behavior had gotten worse. What happened? This was not an issue of skill deficiency or a problem that a one-day training session could solve. This problem required a companywide effort that was not made.

Employee Assistance Program

One of the most effective and least expensive benefit programs is the employee assistance program (EAP), which provides opportunities for employees to obtain counseling for personal problems. Employees' personal problems often spill over into the workplace and affect job performance. Typically, these are alcohol and other drug use and marital problems. The gatekeeper for the EAP is often the employee's supervisor. If the supervisor misunderstands his or her role in the process, the counselors will not be effective. A supervisor should document the work performance problems and not try to assess the personal problem or give advice. The closer the employer integrates its performance and corrective action process with the EAP, the more effective the program will be.

Training is an important investment in the human resources of a company. It requires considerable expense and time commitment. HR professionals need to develop and conduct relevant, reliable, and practical training programs. Evaluating and documenting improvements is just as important as conducting the training.

CHAPTER VIII

MANAGEMENT REPORTS

Everyone has heard speeches praising people as the most important part of a business, but usually employers' actions do not support these words. Human resource professionals encourage management to see a payoff from HR activities, but management often does not see the relationship. The HR professionals may offer excuses: "The payoff is long term" or "You can't measure results in dollars; they're intangible." In human resource circles a common lament is, "The problem is not the program; managers just aren't doing it right."

For a payoff, the first investments must be made in the most needed areas. As business needs change, the investments can be reallocated. A smaller company may need simple recruiting, selection, and orientation services. It might also need basic improvements in recognition and reward strategies or work and staff planning. As the company grows, the need might be training programs and improved communication processes. As administrative activities increase, management wants to know how to control staffing costs and how to achieve more productivity without more people. How does human resources expand its sphere of influence and achieve human resource excellence without being perceived as wasteful?

Human resource functions are successful when three business objectives are achieved: (1) accomplishing the purposes of the employer, (2) supporting other functions interdependently, and (3) returning more in profitability than is expended.

A survey cosponsored by SHRM and Commerce Clearing House found that companies using the "best" human resource practices show a higher degree of productivity and market performance than their competitors. The survey corroborated the findings of similar studies that have shown that effective management practices do make a difference in profitability. Ninety percent of the respondents considered a management philosophy that emphasizes "the importance and value of human resources" to be "very important." But another finding is that a gap exists between practices that are important to a firm's performance and the practices that human resource professionals perceive as important. For example, HR respondents did not consider increased monitoring of the recruiting, hiring, and orientation process as very important; they did not see cultural change and increased diversity in the workforce as a top priority; the majority did not perceive employee assistance or counseling processes as very important; and most HR respondents did not regard safety and employee health as major objectives. Yet survey results showed that these were among the most important indicators of company performance and profitability.

An earlier survey of top managers and CEOs elicited the same kind of responses. The respondents strongly suggested that human resource professionals focus on activities that operating managers do not view as adding value to a company. The findings show that the issues human resource professionals consider important are not considered important by operating managers, and these issues are not the keys to profitability in a company.

The reason for this conflict might be that human resources is not typically perceived as strategic. Instead, management expects human resources to be oriented toward maintenance activities. This perception creates a dilemma between the HR professional's understanding of what needs to be accomplished and top management's purpose in creating the HR function. In these situations, the HR professional must satisfy strategic management objectives while building a foundation of basic human resource activities. If human resources does not identify key objectives, implement activities carefully, and report on its achievements using actual dollar measurements, it will be unable to retain the support of management.

An absolute for successful implementation of a human resource function is following a defined course based on human resource standards, overall management objectives, and company strategies. Despite the stated management objectives, the HR function must start with the basics such as successful recruiting, performance appraisals, and corrective action. Strategic planning, projections, analysis, and organizational change come only after the basic areas are established and operational. Between these two extremes are the usual human resource activities, which may include training and orientation programs, staffing and labor cost control, automating processes, career development, cross-functional processes such as quality and improvement teams, and self-directed work teams. Where to start and how fast to act depend on the company's circumstances and the availability of resources.

When Human Resources Does Not Meet Business Needs

How does the newly appointed human resource professional know which HR management activities are not meeting business needs? As with any other business function, certain signs are present when activities are weak and ineffective. The following are possible signs of problems:

Advanced human resource activities are being conducted without business justification. Many companies and managers, even human resource managers, like to believe they are on the leading edge, because it feeds their professional egos. Management may have initiated excellence in customer service processes, total quality management, manufacturing receiving processes, or a push for the Malcolm Baldrige National Quality Award. However, if managers have not been trained in recruiting, hiring, and EEOC requirements, or there is a high turnover, human resources is not meeting business needs.

There is no budget or control mechanism. Managing expenditures for a maximum payoff is a basic management responsibility and applies to human resources as well. A company that does not do benchmarking—cost-benefit analyses, process payoff inquiries, productivity improvement assessments, or a customer satisfaction survey—is not fulfilling its management role. When a human resource function cannot justify its existence with quantifiable numbers, it will not have the trust and support of top management. Even simple measures, such as figuring out the cost-per-hire and turnover rate of your company and comparing them to costs and rates in other companies, shows management that human resources is attuned to the bottom line.

Nothing seems wrong, but processes are not working. Processes and programs are implemented according to professional standards, but they do not work. An example is a reward and recognition strategy that has no effect on internal inequities. Another is performance standards that are set on arbitrary measurements and not on customer value-added activity. A third example is a recruiting and selection strategy that results in high turnover. The company may have a technically perfect compensation and benefits program, a nationally recognized performance evaluation program, or an expensive recruiting process. But if people are complaining and turnover is high, HR is not doing its job.

There is no payoff from the investment. No matter how technically correct or professionally sophisticated a program is, if it has no payoff, it is useless. The clearest example is that of resources allocated for management and employee training programs that result in no improvements.

Evaluating Management's Effectiveness

Few human resource functions develop a specific HR strategic plan. As discussed in chapter I, they usually participate in companywide strategic planning. Management consultants facilitating the strategic planning process usually find a low priority on human resources and people-oriented strategies and objectives. These are usually folded into general operational objectives. For human resources to be successful, a SWOT (strengths, weaknesses, opportunities, threats) analysis on the work environment should be conducted and specific objectives, strategies, and action plans developed. Trying to start a human resource function without a well-researched and documented strategic plan is, using Peter Drucker's phrase, "trying to do efficiently that which should not be done at all."

Figure VIII-1 shows a sample objective and strategies of a small public sector human resource function. For each of these strategies, the director and staff defined several action plans. For example, the strategy *Increase staff time devoted to providing services to internal clients* might require the action plan shown in **Figure VIII-2**.

Figure VIII-1. Sample HR Function Objective and Strategies

Objective: Improve the efficiency and productivity of the human resources department.

Strategies: Increase staff time devoted to providing services to internal clients.

Automate 25 percent of all transactional processes.

Simplify two work processes by 20 percent each.

Improve internal client satisfaction by 20 percent.

Reduce turnover by 20 percent.

Figure VIII-2. Sample Action Plan

STRATEGY: Increase staff time devoted to providing services to internal clients.

Activities	Responsibility	Completion Date	Resources/ Costs
1. Analyze time by major activity of each staff member. Develop summary report.	Director	1 Jun 96	Staff time
2. Gather data from internal clients re their requirements.	Staff members	15 Jun 96	Staff/client time
3. Brainstorm and prioritize improvement ideas for each staff area.	Team	1 Jul 96	Staff time
4. Set pilot productivity improvement goals for one staff member.	Team	15 Aug 96	Staff time
5. Interim monthly reports @ staff meeting.	Team	Ongoing	Staff time
6. Review/revise plan as necessary.	Team	1 Sep 96	Staff time
7. Identify improvements and calculate cost savings.	Team	1 Dec 96	Staff time
8. Set improvement goals for 1997.	Team	1 Dec 96	Staff time

Increasing staff time dedicated to working with internal clients results in measurable achievements. Is there a cost-improvement justification? If the staff time is spent on activities that add value to the internal client, the answer is obviously yes. Can an actual dollar amount be attached to the savings? Again, the answer is yes.

Human resource professionals use many techniques to identify savings and human resource improvements. Some use a formula based on the cost of adding a salaried professional; others use the value provided to the client; still others might use the improvement in the efficiency of the internal client. Admittedly, these are soft numbers, but even if the statistic is only 50 percent accurate, there still is a considerable return on investment.

The example of increasing staff time devoted to providing services to internal clients might be justified by identifying the number of additional staff required to maintain the same level of service. Human resources might want to focus on value and identify the increased efficiency and satisfaction of the internal client. Identifying money saved when the result is lower turnover or better hiring decisions is also possible. With the true cost of turnover estimated to be from 1.5 to 2.5 times the annual salary of the departing employee, any efforts to reduce turnover will have a rapid return in dollars.

The director of a public sector human resource function used a form similar to that in **Figure VIII-3** to gather data from internal clients. The data were summarized in a monthly report that included comparisons with the same month in the previous year, the previous year's summary, and a current year-to-date summary. The report focused not on numbers, but on areas of improvement and areas in which there was no improvement. The report was distributed to the top management team.

Measuring Management—Organizational Climate Survey

Just as the human resource function should evaluate customer satisfaction based on its internal clients, it should also survey employee satisfaction with the company. Normally this is accomplished using some form of organizational climate (attitude) survey. Two sample questionnaires are included at the end of this chapter **(HRVIII-1.FRM and HRVIII-2.FRM).**

Climate surveys are very popular, but the maximum advantage is seldom gained from them. In fact, management often is surprised at employees' responses and disappointed with the results, because they have unrealistic ideas about how satisfied employees are with the job management is doing. From the employees' point of view, communication of results is not handled very well. Employees are frequently dissatisfied with the priority management places on the identified issues. Organizational climate surveys can be valuable tools, but they regularly fail in use.

Figure VIII-3. Internal Customer/Client Satisfaction Survey

	Satisfied	Somewhat Satisfied	Dissatisfied
1. Did we deliver the service on time?	❑	❑	❑
2. Are you satisfied with the quality of the service?	❑	❑	❑
3. Did we keep you up to date on the service?	❑	❑	❑
4. Did we treat you in a helpful and professional manner?	❑	❑	❑

5. Is there anything else we can do for you? _____

_____

_____

6. Please describe the value our service provided for you. _____

_____

_____

In using an organizational climate survey, the human resource professional should be concerned about the following factors:

- A climate survey should be designed specifically for the company and should include the topics management has the resources to change. Initially at least, topics such as satisfaction with pay and confidence and trust should be avoided. These topics seldom elicit positive responses, because almost all employees believe they deserve more pay and benefits. The quality of supervision also does not usually receive positive ratings from employees.

- Management should be given a comprehensive orientation on the process, feedback mechanisms, and typical responses to each question. This orientation prepares them for the issues employees may identify as serious problems. Managers tend to believe in their infallibility and trust that their subordinates share that belief. Most do not. Unless they are prepared, management may dismiss the results when the survey replies do not meet their expectations.

- The confidential nature of the survey questionnaires and summary responses must be maintained. When employees reveal their honest opinions, they often do not want to be identified with them. In this area, it is crucial that some outside assistance be used. At the very least, an outsider should gather the questionnaires and summarize the data.

- The results of the survey should be discussed with the employees quickly. Any delay will be interpreted by employees as an indication that management and human resources are trying to hide something negative.

- Although many companies use a top-down approach to publishing survey results, consultants and human resource professionals generally find this approach to be inefficient and a barrier to good communication. The more different people interpret the results and feedback, the less accurate the information will be. Also, unless there is stringent monitoring, managers responsible for discussing the survey results often give the process low priority.

- Some companies use norms to benchmark against other companies. First, the biggest disadvantage is that the survey instrument is standardized and thus may include few questions on topics that are of particular interest to an individual company. Second, there is little value in comparing one company with another; the management philosophy, core culture, and work environment will be different. The most valid comparison is benchmarking improvements against previous years' responses. Third, standardized questionnaires usually include 100 to 120 questions. Many respondents will not spend time thinking about their responses to so many questions. And finally, when a standardized questionnaire is used, topics will be included that the company may want to avoid, and employees will then expect management to respond to problems in those areas.

- Human resources should consider each question on a survey instrument to decide if it is properly worded. Unless it is a standardized instrument, human resources should ascertain what each question is asking, what area it addresses, and what the possible responses might be. In this way, there will be no misunderstandings.

A management consultant once said, "Without a yardstick, there is no measurement; without measurement, there is no control." In the first part of this chapter, some ideas were given for measuring human resources and proving that its activities are value-added. Techniques for measuring employee satisfaction with human resources and management were briefly discussed. These are important measurement tools but must be used with care. When conducted casually, without planning and preparation, an organizational climate survey can do more harm than good. Nevertheless, it is one tool that human resources can use to identify and measure its performance and that of management.

Everyone praises people as the most important resource for implementing company strategy. There is a growing need for skilled and educated employees to operate more and more complex technology. As more information is required, employees who can analyze it are essential. Committed employees who can think and make decisions are the difference between competitive success and failure.

Managers in most organizations say that human resource activities are important. But in too many organizations this is just lip service, because managers do not see the payoff from investing in human resource management. In fact, they may believe that, as a staff position, human resources creates no profit but is only an expense. Human resource professionals must show that every HR activity does add value to the company. If this is forgotten, the HR function will quickly fall victim to downsizing and budget restrictions.

Employee Survey
                                                    DATE:

> Note: Read these answer categories carefully, then answer each of the following questions by using the answer number you think is most appropriate. Feel free to make comments in the space below each statement or on the back of the survey.

1.   To what extent is this organization quick to use improved work methods?

2.   To what extent are work activities sensibly organized?

3.   To what extent are decisions made at the levels at which the most adequate and accurate information is available?

4.   To what extent does this organization tell your work group what it needs to know to do the best possible job?

5.   How much does this organization try to improve working conditions?

6.   When decisions are made, to what extent are the persons affected asked for their ideas?

7.   Overall, how satisfied are you with your supervisor?

8.   Overall, how satisfied are you with your job?

9.   To what extent is your supervisor willing to listen to your problems?

10.   To what extent does your supervisor encourage persons in your work group to work as a team?

11.   To what extent does your supervisor encourage people to exchange opinions and ideas?

12.   How much does your supervisor encourage people to give their best effort?

13.   To what extent does your supervisor maintain high levels of performance in the group?

14.   To what extent does your supervisor provide help, training, and guidance so that you can improve your performance?

15.   To what extent does your supervisor ask for opinions and ideas from members of your work group?

16.   To what extent does your supervisor have skills for getting along with others?

17.   To what extent does your supervisor have information about how work group members see and feel about things?

18.   To what extent does your supervisor have an interest in and concern for work group members?

19.   To what extent does your supervisor have confidence and trust in you?

20. To what extent do you have confidence and trust in your supervisor?

21. To what extent does your work group produce the amount of work expected of it?

22. To what extent is your work group efficient in doing the work that is expected of it?

23. To what extent is your work group's work high in quality?

24. How much do persons in your work group encourage each other to work together as a team?

25. How much do persons in your work group emphasize a team goal?

26. How much do persons in your work group exchange ideas and opinions?

27. To what extent do persons in your work group encourage each other to give their best effort?

28. To what extent do persons in your work group maintain high standards of performance?

29. To what extent do persons in your work group help you find ways to do a better job?

30. To what extent do persons in your work group offer each other new ideas for solving job-related problems?

31. To what extent does your work group plan together and coordinate its efforts?

32. To what extent does your work group feel responsible for meeting its objectives successfully?

33. To what extent do you have confidence and trust in the persons in your work group?

34. When conflicts arise between work group members, to what extent are mutually acceptable solutions sought?

35. When solutions are reached, to what extent do the opposing group members accept and implement them?

36. To what extent do you enjoy performing the actual day-to-day activities of your job?

37. To what extent does doing your job give you a sense of personal satisfaction?

38. To what extent does your job let you do a number of different things?

39. To what extent does your job use your skills and abilities—let you do the things you do best?

40. To what extent does doing your job well lead to things like pay increases and bonuses?

41. To what extent does doing your job well lead to things like recognition and respect from those you work with?

42. To what extent does your job provide good chances for getting ahead?

43. To what extent are you clear about what people expect you to do on the job?

44. To what extent do people expect too much from you on your job?

45. To what extent are there times when one person wants you to do one thing and someone else wants you to do something else?

46.   To what extent do you go through a lot of red tape to get things done?

47.   To what extent do you get hemmed in by long-standing rules and regulations that no one seems to be able to explain?

48.   To what extent do different work units plan together and coordinate their efforts?

49.   To what extent does your work unit receive cooperation and assistance from other units?

50.   To what extent do you produce the amount of work that is expected of you?

51.   To what extent are you efficient in doing the work that is expected of you?

52.   To what extent do you produce work that is high in quality?

53.   To what extent is this organization effective in getting you to meet its needs and contribute to its effectiveness?

54.   To what extent does this organization do a good job of meeting your needs as an individual?

55.   Overall, how satisfied are you with this organization?

Employee Questionnaire

We are conducting this attitude survey so that you can state clearly and openly how you feel about your job. If we can find out what our employees think, we can strengthen and improve management policies and management-employee relations and make this company a better place.

DO NOT SIGN YOUR NAME. When you have finished filling out this questionnaire, place it in the locked box provided for all employees. The questionnaires will be tabulated and analyzed and a report will be made to company management summarizing the employee viewpoints expressed in the surveys. This study can be important for your future work happiness...if you are honest and fair in your replies.

Take your time. Please do not confer with your fellow employees as to how you should answer any of the questions.

PART I

In this section of the questionnaire, we would like you to tell us something about yourself. Your answers to these questions will give us the type of information we need to keep our personnel policies current with your needs as employees.

1. My age category:
   - A. 24 and under
   - B. Between 25 and 29
   - C. Between 30 and 39
   - D. 40 or over

2. I have worked for the company approximately the following:
   - A. Under 1 year
   - B. 1 to 4 years
   - C. 5 to 9 years
   - D. Over 9 years

3. I work in the following department:
   - A. Administration
   - B. Packaging
   - C. Fabrication
   - D. Quality Control

4. I am paid:
   - A. Weekly
   - B. Bimonthly

In this section of the questionnaire, we would like you to give us your opinion of your day-to-day activities at work. Your answers to these questions will help provide us with an accurate index of how you feel about your job, your supervisor, and the company. Place an X in the box that best reflects your opinion.

About Your Job

1. How do you like your present job?
   - ☐ A. Don't like it
   - ☐ B. Prefer something else
   - ☐ C. Just accept it, neither liking nor disliking it
   - ☐ D. All things considered, I like it pretty well
   - ☐ E. Like it fine

2. Is the atmosphere of your workplace
   - ☐ A. Extremely hot, cold, drafty, or dusty
   - ☐ B. Usually pleasant
   - ☐ C. Occasionally unpleasant
   - ☐ D. Generally satisfactory
   - ☐ E. Excellent most of the time

3. Is the lighting at your workplace
   - ☐ A. Very bad
   - ☐ B. Poor
   - ☐ C. Just barely good enough
   - ☐ D. All right
   - ☐ E. Just right for the work to be done

4. How about your ability to do your job?
   - ☐ A. I have a lot more ability than my job calls for.
   - ☐ B. My job doesn't make use of many things I can do well.
   - ☐ C. My job makes use of some things I can do well.
   - ☐ D. My job just about fits me.
   - ☐ E. I think I am where I now belong and that my present job will lead to a better one.

5. For the most part, fellow employees in my department are
   - ☐ A. Unfriendly
   - ☐ B. Indifferent to me
   - ☐ C. All right
   - ☐ D. Cooperative
   - ☐ E. Very friendly

6. Compared to other pay rates in the company, do you consider your rate
   - ☐ A. Extremely low
   - ☐ B. On the low side
   - ☐ C. About right
   - ☐ D. Above average
   - ☐ E. Generous

7. How about the chances of getting hurt on your job?
   - ☐ A. There are lots of chances of getting hurt; some could be eliminated.
   - ☐ B. There are still plenty of chances of getting hurt, although the company has eliminated some of them.
   - ☐ C. There is some chance of getting hurt, but it is not bad.
   - ☐ D. Most chances of getting hurt have been eliminated.
   - ☐ E. There is not much chance of getting hurt on my job.

About Your Supervisor

The next seven questions refer to your immediate supervisor.

8. Is your supervisor's attitude toward you personally
   - ☐ A. Always unfair
   - ☐ B. Often unfair
   - ☐ C. Sometimes fair, sometimes not
   - ☐ D. Usually fair
   - ☐ E. Fair at all times

9. If you have a complaint, your supervisor
   - ☐ A. Does nothing about it
   - ☐ B. Usually tries to talk me out of it
   - ☐ C. Passes it on to his boss, but generally nothing happens
   - ☐ D. Listens carefully and acts on complaints that seem valid
   - ☐ E. Accepts all complaints in good spirit, investigates, and gives a clear decision

10. How well does your supervisor keep you informed on company policy, plans, and developments?
    - ☐ A. None of the time
    - ☐ B. Seems not too well-informed himself/herself
    - ☐ C. Informs me some of the time
    - ☐ D. Informs me most of the time
    - ☐ E. Informs me all of the time

11. How well does he or she plan the work of your group?
    - ☐ A. No planning
    - ☐ B. Occasional planning, but not good
    - ☐ C. Tries to plan most of it
    - ☐ D. Plans regularly
    - ☐ E. Plans carefully and systematically

12. How well does he or she explain new things to employees?
    - ☐ A. Never bothers
    - ☐ B. Gives unclear explanations
    - ☐ C. Explains well sometimes
    - ☐ D. Gives clear instructions most of the time
    - ☐ E. Explains carefully and patiently all of the time

13. How well does he or she discipline employees who deserve it?
    - ☐ A. Bawls them out in front of other employees
    - ☐ B. Uses sarcasm in front of other employees
    - ☐ C. Direct, but takes employees aside
    - ☐ D. Criticizes in private, and explains why
    - ☐ E. Always gives helpful criticism and does so in the presence of others

14. I believe my supervisor
    - ☐ A. Is not qualified for the job
    - ☐ B. Lacks some necessary qualifications
    - ☐ C. Is fairly well qualified
    - ☐ D. Is well qualified
    - ☐ E. Is highly qualified

About the Company

15. In comparison with other employers in the community, how well does this company treat its employees?
☐ A. Most others are better
☐ B. A few others are better
☐ C. About as well as the average
☐ D. Our company is better than most
☐ E. Ours is decidedly the best

16. Do you feel that the company
☐ A. Has little genuine regard for employees
☐ B. Looks upon them as workers rather than as human beings
☐ C. Gets by satisfactorily in handling employees
☐ D. Really understands employee problems
☐ E. Shows high regard for the employee's welfare

17. In its relationship with the community, I believe our company
☐ A. Has built ill will
☐ B. Does not have the respect of citizens
☐ C. Should do more than it has
☐ D. Has built some good will
☐ E. Has built a lot of good will

18. When you tell your friends what company you work for, how do you feel?
☐ A. Ashamed to admit it
☐ B. Not happy about it
☐ C. Neutral about it
☐ D. Glad you don't work for certain other companies
☐ E. Proud to tell it

19. In its relations between employees and management, I think the company
☐ A. Is doing a poor job
☐ B. Has considerable room for improvement
☐ C. Is about average
☐ D. Is pretty good
☐ E. Is decidedly outstanding

20. Which one of the following in your opinion shows greatest consideration to employees?
☐ A. Your immediate supervisor
☐ B. Manager of the department
☐ C. Top management of the company

21. Which one of the following in your opinion shows the least consideration to employees?
☐ A. Your immediate supervisor
☐ B. Manager of the department
☐ C. Top management of the company

22. The care and maintenance given to washrooms and toilets is
☐ A. Poor
☐ B. Fair
☐ C. Good

23. The cleanliness of the lunchroom space is
☐ A. Poor
☐ B. Fair
☐ C. Good

24. The food and vending machines are
☐ A. Poor
☐ B. Okay
☐ C. Good

25. Prices at the cafeteria are
☐ A. Entirely too high
☐ B. Okay
☐ C. Reasonable

26. What percentage of profit on sales after paying taxes do you think the company makes?
☐ A. 1%
☐ B. 5%
☐ C. 10%
☐ D. 15%
☐ E. 20% or more

27. What is your opinion of our method of inducting and training new employees?
☐ A. Not enough attention is given to new employees.
☐ B. I have no opinion on this matter.
☐ C. They are being treated well and are properly trained.

28. How much do you think the company has to pay for hospitalization insurance for each employee annually?
☐ A. $50–$99
☐ B. $100–$149
☐ C. $150–$199
☐ D. $200–$249
☐ E. $250 and over

29. Do you feel that prompt action is taken on safety recommendations?
☐ A. No
☐ B. Sometimes
☐ C. Yes

30. Do you frequently receive orders from more than one person?
☐ A. No
☐ B. Yes

31. If you answered yes above, do orders sometimes conflict?
☐ A. No
☐ B. Yes

32. How do you feel about working overtime?
☐ A. Do not like it at all
☐ B. Do not mind it occasionally
☐ C. Neutral about it
☐ D. Like it all the time

Chapter IX

Using Consultants

Society for Human Resource Management

When human resource professionals do not have the answer or do not fully understand the problem, they should immediately seek professional advice. If they are members of the Society for Human Resource Management (SHRM), they have an excellent opportunity for access to accurate, up-to-date information on almost any human resource or employee relations problem. Major benefits include the following:

- **SHRM Information Center.** The information center offers SHRM members a database of articles and information on many topics, access to reference books, and referral services.

- **SHRM *Fast* Facts.** This is a new service offered by SHRM. Members can select from a menu of information and more than 200 documents, including membership applications, SHRM white papers on human resources, annual SHRM conference and exposition information, seminars, lists of publications—even information on international HR. Call (800) 283-7476 for automated services.

- **TeleSHRM.** SHRM's alternative to the traditional membership directory is TeleSHRM. Members can contact colleagues by calling SHRM and asking for the TeleSHRM customer service representatives. The search for a contact can be by title, company name, industry group, professional specialty, geographic location, or any combination of these. Call (800) 770-7476 to access TeleSHRM.

- **SHRM Member Match.** If SHRM members need information from other practitioners, they can obtain members' names by using a Touch-Tone phone to call the SHRM Member Match number. By selecting a subject, they will receive by return fax the names, titles, companies, and telephone numbers of members who have offered to speak about that subject. Call (800) 283-7476 for automated services.

- **SHRM Publications.** SHRM offers the following:

  - *HR Magazine*—This monthly magazine provides in-depth articles; case studies; analyses of employee relations problems; book, product, and service reviews; and a broad-based perspective on human resource management. An added benefit is that advertisers are vendors of some of the best and most used human resource products and services. The magazine often includes special features highlighting consultants and incentive award vendors.

  - *HR News*—This newsletter provides SHRM members with short articles on late-breaking human resource topics, trends, and concerns.

  - *SHRM Legal Reports*—This publication provides quarterly reports on legal issues of interest to human resource professionals.

  - *SHRM Publications Catalog*—The catalog offers many publications on key human resource topics. It includes books, videos, training programs, and subscription newsletters from many publishers. The catalog also offers books published by SHRM and the SHRM Learning System. The reading list in appendix A lists many of these publications.

  - *SHRM Issues in HR*—A special bimonthly report on emerging workplace issues, published by the SHRM Issues Management program.

- **SHRM Seminars and National Conference.** The annual SHRM conference and exposition provides the largest and most focused human resource education opportunity in the world. Session topics include personal growth, human resource strategy, human resource management strategy, practical applications and techniques, and focusing on the future.

SHRM also offers seminars on current human resource topics in major cities throughout the United States and participates with the U.S. Chamber of Commerce in providing Satellite Seminars, which are offered through local chambers of commerce or colleges and universities.

For more information about any of the above or for membership information, contact SHRM member services at (800) 283-7476 by phone or (703) 836-0367 by fax.

Local SHRM Affiliated Chapters

Local SHRM chapters are a valuable resource for the human resource professional, whether just starting or experienced. One major benefit is the chapter roster that local members can use for networking and to get information on techniques and practical applications. Most chapters hold monthly meetings with a speaker on a current human resource topic. Many offer study groups and public seminars, and programs through local college and university continuing education departments. The local chapters are autonomous but operate under general guidelines mandated by SHRM. Membership guidelines vary from chapter to chapter, with some restricting membership to practitioners and others requiring concurrent membership in SHRM. Dues vary by chapter. Contact SHRM for further information and the name of the nearest chapter.

Using Local Human Resource Professionals

Although often not considered a resource, many experienced human resource professionals are happy to help new members of the profession advance their careers and develop practical experience. Generally, those who have practiced longest are most proficient in providing realistic advice and help. This source of advice can be extremely helpful because most of these professionals did not get their expertise out of a book or by attending classes; they learned on the line. They can offer valuable strategic advice, help newcomers to the field avoid mistakes and wasted effort, and help in developing a practical human resource function.

Hiring a Consultant

For the purposes of this discussion, lawyers, accountants, and academics are considered consultants. The term "consultant" is the butt of many jokes: "A consultant is someone who borrows the client's watch to tell the client the time"; "...someone out of work with a briefcase and 50 miles from home"; "...a lawyer who rescues your estate from your enemies to keep it for himself." The consulting profession is poorly understood, and anticipated results vary considerably. By defining the role of a consultant, the human resource professional can better understand how to use consultants' services and obtain superior outcomes. This section discusses what consultants do, how to decide whether you need one, how to choose a consultant, and how to work with him or her.

What Does a Consultant Do?

A consultant renders advice and services in a professional or technical skill area *at some fixed fee or on a contractual basis.* Consultants give advice or complete a specific project for an agreed-upon fee. They should be able to clarify the boundaries of the client's felt need and sometimes even to familiarize the client with the structure of the problem. When clients have not planned the essential activities or the required outcomes, there may be misunderstandings, conflicts, and unsuccessful results. How can human resources be more successful in working with consultants?

Understanding what a consultant can and cannot do is essential. For example, a common management complaint is that external pay inequity is causing internal problems. When there is a positive work environment and employees trust the decisions of management, pay is usually not an issue. When management practices are poor and a "we-they" work environment exists, complaints about pay are usually a symptom, not the real problem.

If the consultant develops a pay plan based on external equity, even if this is management's objective, turnover and complaints will not decrease. The company will have wasted the consultant's fee, the time employees spent on the project, and the additional pay. Every succeeding year, the company will lose the opportunity for increased productivity and still have to pay. On the other hand, if the consultant is asked to advise on how the employer can create a positive work environment, he or she may consider not only pay but also the recruiting and selection process, nonfinancial reward and recognition procedures, and the amount and type of supervisory training.

Deciding If a Consultant Is Needed

Most human resource practitioners have good experiences working with consultants, but some have had serious problems. When the client is responsible for the failure, it is usually a result of not doing the proper planning, not understanding the consulting industry, or not communicating clearly with the consultant. **Figure IX-1** lists some arguments for and against using a consultant.

Figure IX-1. Arguments For and Against Hiring a Consultant

For
- Skills not available in-house
- Don't have the time in-house
- Need outside perspective
- Don't know what needs to be done
- Need a second opinion
- Consultant may be more efficient
- Short-term project

Against
- Company may not be receptive
- Not ready to hear bad news
- Support resources not available in-house
- Not the right time

Based on *Selecting and Working with Consultants*

Many companies decide to start a human resource function and expect it to be fully functional in 30 days. The person starting a human resource function may have all the necessary technical skills, but implementation can be extremely tedious and difficult. A consultant can be extremely helpful in getting the process off to the right start quickly. Finally, the human resource function is a process that encompasses times of extremely high activity and lulls. In the initial stages of a human resource function, management will provide more support and commitment if human resources is perceived as frugal and thrifty. Hiring a consultant is an effective technique for controlling staffing needs.

Before hiring a consultant, some possible problems should be considered. See **Figure IX-2**. Human resource professionals should address problems fully, because if a consultant is hired and the project fails or does not meet expectations, there will usually be long-term consequences.

The Consulting Process

Once it is decided to bring a consultant in to help on a project, the human resource professional should do some planning. **Figure IX-3** outlines recommended steps in working with a consultant.

A Final Word on Getting Advice and Using Consultants

Most human resource professionals, even experienced generalists, will need outside assistance at times. HR professionals, especially in large companies, often have a staff or a network of peers who regularly discuss common problems. For the newly appointed human resource professional, getting advice and assistance has clear advantages, whether it is through other experienced HR professionals, or by tapping into the advice and assistance of competent consultants.

Although a discussion of consulting has taken most of this chapter, it does not mean a consultant is necessary. Most human resource functions have been developed with small consulting assistance. Using consultants has many advantages. Consultants offer advice and assistance in most human resource skill areas. Still, using consultants does present some risks. The objective of this chapter was to give the newly appointed human resource professional an overview on how to use consultants and then in stages lead the reader through the process.

Figure IX-2. Problems and Solutions in Hiring a Consultant

Problem	Solution
Manager dominates the consultant and insists on doing things the same way.	Hire a consultant with the courage and skills to challenge the status quo.
General reluctance to use a consultant.	Have the consultant prepare a cost-benefit analysis. Start consultant on pilot projects to test fit and build trust. Get references from other clients.
Loss of employee commitment.	Involve employees from the start and communicate with them.
Hiring the wrong consultant.	Insist on a consultant with a blend of general knowledge and practical experience. Get references.
Bailing out too quickly when problems arise.	Ensure frequent progress meetings with consultant. Give early feedback.
Lack of financial resources.	Negotiate the consultant's fee as a percentage of savings. Stage the project over time.

Figure IX-3. Consulting Project Flowchart

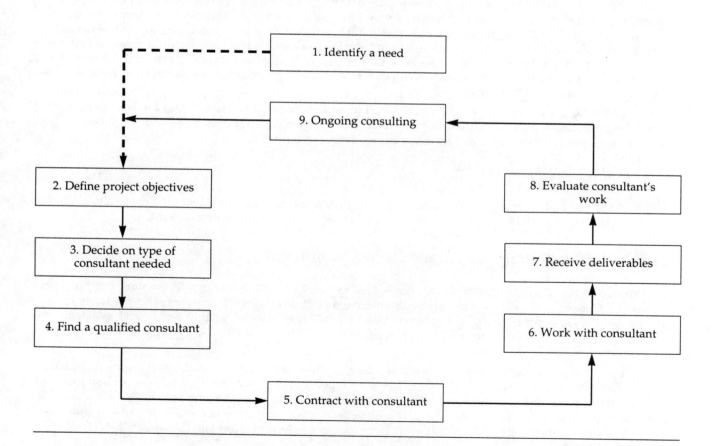

Appendix A

Resources and Reading List

Training Programs with Videos

Coaching and Counseling, Minor, M., Crisp Publications, Inc., Los Altos, CA

Conducting Lawful Terminations, Coleman, F.T., SHRM, Alexandria, VA, 1995

Effective Performance Evaluations, Maddux, R., Crisp Publications, Inc., Los Altos, CA, 1995

How to Avoid Costly Hiring Mistakes, SHRM, Alexandria, VA, 1995

New Supervisor, Chapman, E.N., Crisp Publications, Inc., Los Altos, CA

SHRM Learning System, SHRM, Alexandria, VA, 1995

SHRM's Strategic HR Management Series, SHRM, Alexandria, VA, 1995

10 Steps to Successful Job Orientation, SHRM, Alexandria: VA, 1995

Workers Compensation-ADA Connection, Pimental, R.K., Bell, C.G., Esq, Smith, G.M., MD, and Larson, H.J. Milt Wright and Associates, Chatworth, CA, 1993.

SHRM-BNA Series on HR Management

Human Resource Management: Evolving Roles and Responsibilities—Volume 1, Dryer, E., ed., SHRM and BNA, Alexandria, VA, 1988

Human Resource Planning, Employment and Placement—Volume 2, Casio, W., ed., SHRM and BNA, Alexandria, VA, 1989

Compensation and Benefits—Volume 3, Gomez-Mejia, L.R., ed., SHRM and BNA, Alexandria, VA, 1989

Employee and Labor Relations—Volume 4, Possum, J.A., ed., SHRM and BNA, Alexandria, VA, 1990

Developing Human Resources—Volume 5, Wexley, K.N., ed., SHRM and BNA, Alexandria, VA, 1990

Managing Human Resources in the Information Age—Volume 6, Schuler, R.S., ed., SHRM and BNA, Alexandria, VA, 1991

Other Resources

America: What Went Wrong, Barlett, D.L., Steele, J.B., Andrews and McMeel, Kansas City, MO, 1992

Before It's Too Late: Employee Involvement...An Idea Whose Time Has Come, Grazier, P.B., Teambuilding Inc., Chadds Ford, PA, 1989

The BLR Handbook of Minimum Wage and Overtime Regulation, Business and Legal Reports, Madison, CT, 1989, updates

Compensation, Milkovich, G.T., Newman, J.M., BPI Irwin, Homewood, IL, 1987

Dr. Deming: The American Who Taught the Japanese About Quality, Aguayo, R., Fireside, New York, 1991

Effective Human Resource Measurement Techniques, SHRM Research Committee, SHRM, Alexandria, VA, 1990

Eternally Successful Organization, Crosby, P.B., McGraw Hill, Inc., New York, 1988

The Eternally Successful Organization, Crosby, P., NAL-Dutton, New York, 1992

The Federal Wage and Hour Laws, Dixon R.B., SHRM, Alexandria, VA, 1994

Forecasting Financial Benefits of Human Resource Development, Swanson, R.A., Gradous, D.B., Jossey-Bass Publishers, San Francisco and Oxford, 1990

Handbook of Training Evaluation and Measurement Methods, Phillips, J.J., Gulf Publishing Company, Houston, 1991

Hiring the Best: A Manager's Guide to Effective Interviewing, Yate, M.J., Bob Adams, Inc., Holbrook, MA, 1994

How To Conduct Training Seminars: A Complete Reference Guide for Training Managers and Professionals, Monson, L.S., McGraw Hill, Inc., New York, 1992

Human Resource Financial Report, Saratoga Institute, Saratoga, CA, 1995 (annual)

Kaizen: Key to Japan, Imai, M., McGraw-Hill, New York, 1986

Keeping the Best, and Other Thoughts on Building a Super-Competitive Workforce, Yate, M.J., Bob Adams, Inc., Holbrook, MA, 1991

Legal Environment of Business, Blackburn, J.D., Klayman, E.I., Malin, M.H., Richard D. Irwin, Inc., Homewood, IL, and Boston, 1991

New Pay: Linking Employee and Organizational Performance, Schuster, J.R., Zingheim, P.K., Lexington Books, New York, 1992

Quality Is Free, Crosby, P., NAL-Dutton, New York, 1980

Running Things: The Art of Making Things Happen, Crosby, P., McGraw-Hill, New York, 1989

Seven Habits of Highly Effective People, Covey, S.R., Fireside, New York, 1990

Strategic Planning: What Every Manager Must Know, Steiner, G.A., The Free Press, New York, 1979

The Terrible Truth About Lawyers: What I Should Have Learned at Yale Law School, McCormack, M.H., Avon, New York, 1988

Total Quality, An Executive's Guide for the '90s, Ernst & Young Quality Improvement Group, Irwin Prof. Publishing, Burr Ridge, IL, 1989

Worklife Visions: Redefining Work for the Information Economy, Hallett, J.J., SHRM, Alexandria, VA, 1989

ZAPP! The Lightning of Empowerment, Byham, W.C., Crown Publishing Group, New York, 1990

APPENDIX B

FEDERAL LEGISLATION AFFECTING HUMAN RESOURCES

The following are summaries of laws that affect human resources. For specific questions, see the actual regulations or seek the advice of a consultant or employment lawyer. *SHRM Legal Reports*, quarterly reports on legal issues, contain more information. Call (800) 283-7476 for SHRM automated services.

The **National Labor Relations Act (NLRA)**, enacted in 1935 as a result of the lack of job security in companies and increase in unionism, protects the rights of employees to join unions and bargain collectively. It applies to employers in all industries affecting commerce and to all employees except agricultural laborers, domestic employees or individuals employed by their families, independent contractors, and supervisors. It prohibits employers from certain unfair labor practices. Primary responsibility for enforcement is vested in the National Labor Relations Board (NLRB). The decisions of the NLRB form the provisions under which the labor-management structure operates. The **Taft-Hartley Act (Labor-Management Relations Act)** was passed in 1947 in response to the belief that unions had become too strong and that employers needed some protection. It modified some of the pro-union provisions of the NLRA and prohibits certain unfair labor practices by unions. The Taft-Hartley Act allows the president to declare a national emergency if a strike significantly impairs the national health and safety. Such a declaration delays the strike up to 80 days and starts a process designed to end it. The **Landum-Griffin Act (Labor-Management Reporting and Disclosure Act)** was passed in 1959 as a result of a congressional committee's finding of union corruption. It protects the rights of individual union members. These three laws constitute the basis of what is termed the "National Labor Code."

The **Fair Labor Standards Act of 1938 (FLSA)** is the broadest piece of employee relations legislation in the United States. It regulates the status of employees (versus independent contractors) and provides for a minimum wage and overtime unless the employee is exempt. (For more information, see *Federal Wage and Hour Laws*, published by SHRM in 1994. The **Equal Pay Act of 1963** is technically an amendment to FLSA and prohibits wage discrimination by requiring equal pay for equal work. A prima facie case occurs when an employee shows that she or he receives a lower wage than a member of the opposite sex for work that requires substantially the same skills, effort, and responsibilities under similar working conditions.

The **Age Discrimination Employment Act of 1978 (ADEA)** prohibits discrimination in employment for persons 40 and over. Amendments in 1978 and 1986 first raised and then eliminated the age at which an employee could be forced to retire. This act covers all private and public employers with 20 or more employees, unions with 25 or more members, employment agencies, and apprenticeship and training programs.

Title VII of the Civil Rights Act of 1964 prohibits discrimination in all terms and conditions of employment (including pay and benefits) on the basis of race, religion, ethnic group, sex, or national origin. It requires that all persons of the same skills, seniority, and background be treated similarly. Title VII was amended in 1972, 1978, and 1991. The act makes specific employment practices unlawful. Title VII is administered by the Equal Employment Opportunity Commission (EEOC), and employees must file a charge of discrimination with the EEOC or a state agency before filing a private suit. Even if the EEOC finds there is no probable cause for believing discrimination exists, it will issue a right to sue letter, which allows the employee to initiate a private lawsuit against the employer.

If employers use non-job related and discriminatory personnel practices, they are liable for the resulting employee relations liability. The 1972 amendment expanded coverage to include employees of government and educational institutions and private sector employers with 15 or more employees. The 1978 amendment made it illegal to discriminate on the basis of pregnancy, childbirth, or related conditions.

The 1991 amendment creates new damage awards for intentional (disparate treatment) discrimination claims by disabled workers and by those who claim discrimination on the basis of their sex, religion, color, or national origin if these are not covered by Section 1981 of Title VII. Finally the act creates the right to demand a jury trial in cases in which the new damage awards are sought. Employees proving intentional acts of discrimination may recover compensatory and punitive damages in addition to the traditional remedies. To recover, the employee must prove that the employer acted with "malice or with reckless indifference" to the employee's rights. The sum of compensatory and punitive damages may not exceed the following:

Number of employees	Maximum dollar recovery
15–100	$50,000
101–200	$100,000
201–500	$200,000
Over 500	$300,000

The 1991 amendment addressed a variety of other issues. It negated a number of "employer-friendly" U.S. Supreme Court decisions made between 1988 and 1990. Consequently, employers need to be very confident that their actions are job-related and based on business necessity.

The **Uniform Guidelines on Employee Selection (1978)** for carrying out Title VII of the Civil Rights Act state that selection policies or practices that have an adverse impact on the employment opportunities for any race, sex, or ethnic group are considered discriminatory—and therefore illegal—unless business necessity can justify them. It defines "adverse impact."

The **Consumer Credit Protection Act of 1968** sets a national maximum limit on the amount of an employee's wages that can be withheld to satisfy a wage garnishment. The act also restricts the right of employers to discharge employees whose pay is subjected to a single garnishment order. All 50 states also have laws that restrict the employer's right to discipline or terminate an employee because of wage garnishments; if the state law sets a lower maximum, that applies. Federal and state tax debts are exempt from the provisions of this act.

The **Fair Credit Reporting Act (1970)** requires employers to inform applicants in writing that they will conduct an inquiry into the applicant's financial status. Applicants must be informed if they are denied employment because of information obtained during the inquiry and must be given the name and address of the third party who investigated them.

The **Vocational Rehabilitation Act (1973)**, amended in 1980, prevents employment discrimination against people who have physical or mental disabilities. The act requires federal contractors who have contracts of more than $2,500 to "take affirmative action to employ and advance disabled individuals" at all levels of employment, including jobs at the executive level.

The **Vietnam-Era Veterans' Readjustment Assistance Act of 1974** was enacted as a result of concerns about the readjustment of Vietnam-era veterans into the workforce at the end of the military action. The act requires that affirmative action in hiring and promotion be undertaken by government contractors and subcontractors with contracts of more than $10,000.

The **Privacy Act (1974)** prohibits federal agencies from revealing certain information without permission from employees. The act gives employees the right to inspect records about themselves held by the federal government and to make corrections and copies.

The **Employee Retirement Income Security Act (1974)** was the result of widespread criticism of pension plans. The purpose of the law and subsequent amendments was to set standards and requirements for the administration of employee benefit and welfare plans, to ensure that employees who put money in a pension plan for retirement will actually receive the money. The act also requires employers to cover part-time workers who work more than 1,000 hours a year and to submit annual pension-reporting statements to employees.

The **Military Selective Service Act (1974)** protects all employees who are inducted into the armed forces and requires the employer to restore the employee to a position of like seniority, status, and pay if the employee returns to work within 90 days of discharge. For employees in the military reserve, the act requires the employer to grant an annual leave of absence to permit the employee to participate in active duty.

The **Immigration and Naturalization Act (1966)** covers the hiring of resident aliens and new or prospective immigrants. A more recent law, the **Immigration Reform and Control Act of 1986 (IRCA)**, amended in 1990, requires that new hires provide specific documents to employers showing that they are who they claim to be and that they have the legal right to work in the United States. The burden of verifying that a new employee is eligible to work in the United States falls on the employer. The employee must complete Form 1-9, and an authorized representative of the employer must verify that the information presented is correct. The I-9s must be retained at the location where the employee actually works for review by federal compliance officers, should an inspection occur. The forms must be retained for three years from the date of hire until one year after termination. Employers who violate this law are subject to civil, and in some cases criminal, penalties.

IRCA also makes it illegal for employers to discriminate on the basis of national origin, citizenship, or intention to obtain citizenship to the extent the discriminating behavior is not covered by the Civil Rights Act of 1964.

The **Americans with Disabilities Act (1990) (ADA)** protects qualified individuals with disabilities from unlawful discrimination in employment, public services and transportation, public accommodations, and telecommunication services. Discrimination is prohibited against individuals if they can do the essential job functions with reasonable proficiency. An employer must make *reasonable accommodations* (without compromising safety) for persons with disabilities unless doing so would place *undue hardship* upon the employer. The emphasized words may have different meanings with different employers.

According to the **Drug-Free Workplace Act (1988)**, firms that do business with the federal government must have written drug-use policies. Federal contractors with contracts of $25,000 or more must follow certain requirements to certify that they maintain a drug-free workplace. They must issue a statement prohibiting the illegal manufacture, distribution, dispensation, possession, or use of any controlled substances in the workplace and specify the consequences for violating the policy. The employer must establish a drug abuse awareness process for informing employees about the dangers of drug abuse, explaining the employer's policy and the availability of employee assistance programs, and specifying the action that will be taken if an employee is convicted of a drug violation occurring in the workplace.

The **Worker Adjustment and Retraining Notification Act of 1988 (WARN)** requires employers to give notice of plant closings. Employers of 100 or more employees must provide 60 days' advance notice of a plant closing that will cause an employment loss for 50 or more employees within any 30-day period. The employer must also give notice if there will be a layoff within any 30-day period for one-third of the workforce and at least 50 employees or for 500 or more employees at a single worksite. The act does not require the employer to count as affected employees retirees, employees discharged for cause, and those who accept transfers to another worksite. The notice is required to be given to the union that represents the employees or, if they are not represented, to each employee, to the state unemployment office, and to the official who heads the local government subdivision.

The **Older Workers Benefit Protection Act (OWBPA) of 1990** amends ADEA and requires equal treatment for older workers in retirement and severance situations. It sets forth the specific criteria that must be met when older workers sign waivers not to sue for age discrimination. Basically, employers should have two separately worded severance agreements, one for employees under 40 years old and one for those 40 and over. In addition, benefits provided for older workers must be of "equal benefit or equal cost" to those provided for other workers. Employers may, in certain situations, make deductions from severance benefits (offsets). Finally, the employer may deduct the value of any postretirement health benefits from severance benefits.

Executive Order 11246 requires federal contractors with contracts of more than $10,000 to comply with Title VII; they must not discriminate on the basis of race, color, religion, sex, or national origin. In addition, federal contractors with contracts of more than $50,000 and 50 or more employees must develop a written affirmative action plan to increase the workforce participation of members of protected classes.

Although some people have stated that the use of affirmative action to remedy underrepresentation of members of protected classes is really a form of quotas, the **Civil Rights Act of 1991** specifically prohibits the use of quotas. Some people equate affirmative action with hiring unqualified or less qualified individuals and with reverse discrimination. The Executive Order does not require the hiring of less qualified women and minorities; in conjunction with the Civil Rights Act, it requires that only job-related characteristics be used in making personnel decisions. The consequence is that hiring criteria, promotion opportunities, and compensation practices that favor the majority and that cause an "adverse impact" on females and minorities can no longer be used.

In response to violations of the Executive Order, the secretary of labor has the power to do the following:

- Cancel federal contracts and bar the company from further contracts.
- Recommend action by the Equal Employment Opportunity Commission.
- Publish names of firms not in compliance.

In addition to the specific requirements of Executive Orders 11246, 11375, and 11478, federal contractors must comply with all EEO regulations and guidelines.

The **Family and Medical Leave Act (FMLA) of 1993** covers employers with 50 or more employees located within 75 miles of a workplace and includes federal, state, and private employers. Employees who have worked 12 months or 1,250 hours in the previous year are eligible for leave under FMLA. They may take up to 12 weeks' leave during any 12-month period for one of the following reasons:

- Birth, adoption, or foster care of a child.
- Caring for a spouse, child, or parent who has a serious health condition.
- Serious health condition of the employee.

A serious health condition is one requiring inpatient, hospital, hospice, or residential medical care or continuing medical care.

Employers may apply accrued paid vacation, personal, and sick leave toward the 12-week leave.

Employees may be required to apply this leave to the mandated 12 weeks, but they may take the leave on an intermittent or reduced schedule, when medically necessary. Employees are entitled to health benefits during the leave as if they had been at work.

If the employer violates the employee's rights under FMLA, the employee may recover actual monetary losses with interest. Employees may seek equitable relief such as reinstatement or promotion.